Anne Childs.

Killers
OF THE
Dream

Books by Lillian Smith

STRANGE FRUIT
KILLERS OF THE DREAM

LILLIAN SMITH

Killers
OF THE
Dream

W · W · NORTON & COMPANY · INC · New York

IN MEMORY OF
my Mother and Father

Contents

8 CONTENTS

Foreword

THIS BOOK is addressed to men and women who are concerned with the continued existence of an earth trembling between past and future. Hard, bitter facts of life are discussed in it that neither children nor fools can be nourished on. I have written as plainly as one talks to one's family in crisis, uncovering experiences which our health as human beings requires us to understand.

I hope that it is an honest book, and that it will bring back not dust and spiderwebs but important things that we need to know, from its search into the dark corners of a past which we have locked our minds in. I would like to believe also that it is written with the affection I feel for our people who in their flight from trouble only carry it with them wherever they go.

It is a story made of memory and historical fact. I have reached into the past for both and blended them with the present. For, as time swirls through a man's life without end or beginning, so in a people's common experiences yesterday's incident is lost to view as a century-old happening looms suddenly before them.

I have been more concerned with fears than with figures, more with the curve of an idea as it moves from father to child than with dates, more with the quality of feeling behind a fact than with the fact itself, and as much with the child as the man he grew into. The authorities on whom I have leaned most heavily for the few figures and dates, names and places I have used, are Gunnar Myrdal's *American Dilemma;* Arthur Raper and Ira De A. Reid's *Sharecroppers All;* H. C. Nixon's *Forty Acres and Steel Mules;* Rupert Vance's *Human Geography of the South;* Charles Johnson's *Patterns of Negro Segregation;* Odum's *Southern Regions;* Paul Buck's *Road to Reunion;* Carey McWilliams' *Brothers under the Skin;* Liston Pope's *Millhands and Preachers;* and the *Negro Year Book* by M. N. Work. Recent statistics on expenditures for colored and white schools in the South are those released by the U.S. Office of Education. Quotations have their sources in the Atlanta *Constitution,* Atlanta *Journal,* in *Events and Trends in Race Relations,* and in W. J. Cash's *Mind of the South.* The interpretations of facts, the generalizations, are my own. I have not cited specific instances from them, but I have learned much about race relations from Gilberto Freyre's *The Master and the Slaves,* John Dollard's *Caste and Class in a Southern Town,* Franklin Frazer's *The Negro Family in the United States,* Hortense Powdermaker's *After Freedom,* James Weldon Johnson's *Along This Way,* Walter White's *A Man Named White* and from the writings of Richard Wright and W. E. B. DuBois, as well as from my own observations as a southerner.

Though I owe a heavy debt to my mother and father for my beliefs as well as to the unnumbered novelists, poets, dramatists, historians, philosophers I have read since childhood, in more recent years I have listened closely to the words of such men as Sigmund Freud, Karl Menninger,

Sandor Ferenczi, Hanns Sachs, Géza Róheim, Horace Kallen, José Ortega y Gasset, Albert Schweitzer, and Gandhi as I have tried to form my views about this world we live in. These are influences that cannot be measured, and I shall not try to do so.

Nor can I measure the debt of gratitude which I owe Paula Snelling, with whom I have worked for so many years as co-director of a camp for children, as co-editor of *South Today*, for her insight, her critical intelligence, her painstaking fact-finding, her never-failing encouragement as I made the slow and painful return journey to the memories of my childhood in an attempt to find the answer to that old question that gnaws on every mind: Why has the white man dreamed so fabulous a dream of freedom and human dignity and again and again tried to kill his own dream?

Lillian Smith

Clayton, Georgia

~ Part One ~

The Dreamers

❧ 1 ❧

When I Was a Child

EVEN ITS children know
that the South is in trouble. No one has to tell them; no
words said aloud. To them, it is a vague thing weaving in
and out of their play, like a ghost haunting an old graveyard or whispers after the household sleeps—fleeting mystery, vague menace, to which each responds in his own way.
Some learn to screen out all except the soft and the soothing;
others deny even as they see plainly, and hear. But all know
that under quiet words and warmth and laughter, under
the slow ease and tender concern about small matters, there
is a heavy burden on all of us and as heavy a refusal to confess it. The children know this "trouble" is bigger than they,
bigger than their family, bigger than their church, so big
that people turn away from its size. They have seen it flash
out like lightning and shatter a town's peace, have felt it
tear up all they believe in. They have measured its giant
strength and they feel weak when they remember.

This haunted childhood belongs to every southerner.
Many of us run away from it but we come back like a hurt
animal to its wound, or a murderer to the scene of his sin.

The human heart dares not stay away too long from that which hurt it most. There is a return journey to anguish that few of us are released from making.

We who were born in the South call this mesh of feeling and memory "loyalty." We think of it sometimes as "love." We identify with the South's trouble as if we, individually, were responsible for all of it. We defend the sins and sorrows of three hundred years as if each sin had been committed by us alone and each sorrow had cut across our heart. We are as hurt at criticism of our region as if our own name were called aloud by the critic. We have known guilt without understanding it, and there is no tie that binds men closer to the past and each other than that.

It is a strange thing, this umbilical cord uncut. In times of ease, we do not feel its pull, but when we are threatened with change, suddenly it draws the whole white South together in a collective fear and fury that wipe our minds clear of reason and we are blocked off from sensible contact with the world we live in.

To keep this resistance strong, wall after wall has been thrown up in the southern mind against criticism from without and within. Imaginations close tight against the hurt of others; a regional armoring takes place to keep out the "enemies" who would make our trouble different—or maybe rid us of it completely. For it is a trouble that we do not want to give up. We are as involved with it as a child who cannot be happy at home and cannot bear to tear himself away, or as a grown-up who has fallen in love with his own disease. We southerners have identified with the long sorrowful past on such deep levels of love and hate and guilt that we do not know how to break old bonds without pulling our lives down. *Change* is the evil word, a shrill clanking that makes us know too well our servitude. *Change* means leaving one's memories, one's sins, one's ancient prison, the room where one was born. How can we do this when we are tied fast!

The white man's burden is his own childhood. Every southerner knows this. Though he may deny it even to himself, yet he drags through life with him the heavy weight of a past that never eases and is rarely understood, of desire never appeased, of dreams that died in his heart.

In this South I was born and now live. Here it was that I began to grow, seeking my way, as do all children, through the honeycomb cells of our life to the bright reality outside. Sometimes it was as if all doors opened inward. . . . Sometimes we children lost even the desire to get outside and tried only to make a comfortable home of the trap of swinging doors that history and religion and a war, man's greed and his guilt had placed us in at birth.

It is not easy to pick out of such a life those strands that have to do only with color, only with Negro-white relationships, only with religion or sex, for they are knit of the same fibers that have gone into the making of the whole fabric, woven into its basic patterns and designs. Religion . . . sex . . . race . . . money . . . avoidance rites . . . malnutrition . . . dreams—no part of these can be looked at and clearly seen without looking at the whole of them. For, as a painter mixes colors and makes of them new colors, so religion is turned into something different by race, and segregation is colored as much by sex as by skin pigment, and money is no longer a coin but a lost wish wandering through a man's whole life.

A child's lessons are blended of these strands however dissonant a design they make. The mother who taught me what I know of tenderness and love and compassion taught me also the bleak rituals of keeping Negroes in their place.

The father who rebuked me for an air of superiority toward schoolmates from the mill and rounded out his rebuke by gravely reminding me that "all men are brothers," trained me in the steel-rigid decorums I must demand of every colored male. They who so gravely taught me to split my body from my feelings and both from my "soul," taught me also to split my conscience from my acts and Christianity from southern tradition.

Neither the Negro nor sex was often discussed at length in our home. We were given no formal instruction in these difficult matters but we learned our lessons well. We learned the intricate system of taboos, of renunciations and compensations, of manners, voice modulations, words, feelings, along with our prayers, our toilet habits, and our games. I do not remember how or when, but by the time I had learned that God is love, that Jesus is His Son and came to give us more abundant life, that all men are brothers with a common Father, I also knew that I was better than a Negro, that all black folks have their place and must be kept in it, that sex has its place and must be kept in it, that a terrifying disaster would befall the South if ever I treated a Negro as my social equal and as terrifying a disaster would befall my family if ever I were to have a baby outside of marriage. I had learned that God so loved the world that He gave His only begotten Son so that we might have segregated churches in which it was my duty to worship each Sunday and on Wednesday at evening prayers. I had learned that white southerners are a hospitable, courteous, tactful people who treat those of their own group with consideration and who as carefully segregate from all the richness of life "for their own good and welfare" thirteen million people whose skin is colored a little differently from my own.

I knew by the time I was twelve that a member of my family would always shake hands with old Negro friends, would speak gently and graciously to members of the Negro race unless they forgot their place, in which event icy peremptory tones would draw lines beyond which only the desperate would dare take one step. I knew that to use the word "nigger" was unpardonable and no well-bred southerner was quite so crude as to do so; nor would a well-bred southerner call a Negro "mister" or invite him into the living room or eat with him or sit by him in public places.

I knew that my old nurse who had patiently cared for me through long months of illness, who had given me refuge when a little sister took my place as the baby of the family, who comforted me, soothed, fed me, delighted me with her stories and games, let me fall asleep on her deep warm breast, was not worthy of the passionate love I felt for her but must be given instead a half-smiled-at affection similar to that which one feels for one's dog. I knew but I never believed it, that the deep respect I felt for her, the tenderness, the love, was a childish thing which every normal child outgrows, that such love begins with one's toys and is discarded with them, and that somehow—though it seemed impossible to my agonized heart—I too, must outgrow these feelings. I learned to give presents to this woman I loved, instead of esteem and honor. I learned to use a soft voice to oil my words of superiority. I learned to cheapen with tears and sentimental talk of "my old mammy" one of the profound relationships of my life. I learned the bitterest thing a child can learn: that the human relations I valued most were held cheap by the world I lived in.

From the day I was born, I began to learn my lessons. I was put in a rigid frame too intricate, too complex, too twisting to describe here so briefly, but I learned to conform to its slide-rule measurements. I learned that it is possible to be a Christian and a white southerner simultaneously; to be a gentlewoman and an arrogant callous creature in the same moment; to pray at night and ride a Jim Crow car the next morning and to feel comfortable in doing both. I learned to believe in freedom, to glow when the word *democracy* is used, and to practice slavery from morning to night. I learned it the way all of my southern people learn it: by closing door after door until one's mind and heart and conscience are blocked off from each other and from reality.

I closed the doors. Or perhaps they were closed for me. Then one day they began to open again. Why I had the desire or the strength to open them or what strange accident or circumstance opened them for me would require in the answering an account too long, too particular, too stark to make here. And perhaps I should not have the insight or wisdom that such an analysis would demand of me, nor the will to make it. I know only that the doors opened, a little; that somewhere along that iron corridor we travel from babyhood to maturity, doors swinging inward began to swing outward, showing glimpses of the world beyond, of that clear bright thing we call "reality."

I believe there is one experience in my childhood which pushed these doors open, a little. And I am going to tell it here, although I know well that to excerpt from a life and family background one incident and name it as a "cause" of a change in one's life direction is a distortion and often an irrelevance. The profound hungers of a child and how they are filled have too much to do with the way in which experiences are assimilated to tear an incident out of a life and look at it in isolation. Yet, with these reservations, I shall tell it, not be-

cause it was in itself so severe a trauma, but because it became for me a symbol of buried experiences that I did not
have access to. It is an incident that has rarely happened to
other southern children. In a sense, it is unique. But it was
an acting-out, a special private production of a little script
that is written on the lives of most southern children before
they know words. Though they may not have seen it staged
this way, each southerner has had his own dramatization of
the theme.

I should like to preface the account by giving a brief
glimpse of my family and background, hoping that the
reader, entering my home with me, will be able to blend
the ragged edges of this isolated experience into a more full
life picture and in doing so will see that it is, in a sense,
everybody's story.

I was born and reared in a small Deep South town whose
population was about equally Negro and white. There were
nine of us who grew up freely in a rambling house of many
rooms, surrounded by big lawn, back yard, gardens, fields,
and barn. It was the kind of home that gathers memories
like dust, a place filled with laughter and play and pain and
hurt and ghosts and games. We were given such advantages
of schooling, music, and art as were available in the South,
and our world was not limited to the South, for travel to
far places seemed a simple, natural thing to us, and usually
there was one of the family in a remote part of the earth.

We knew we were a respected and important family of
this small town but beyond this knowledge we gave little
thought to status. Our father made money in lumber and
naval stores for the excitement of making and losing it—
not for what money can buy nor the security which it sometimes gives. I do not remember at any time wanting "to be
rich" nor do I remember that thrift and saving were ideals

which our parents considered important enough to urge upon us. Always in the family there was an acceptance of risk, a mild delight even in burning bridges, an expectant "what will happen now!" We were not irresponsible; living according to the pleasure principle was by no means our way of life. On the contrary we were trained to think that each of us should do something that would be of genuine usefulness to the world, and the family thought it right to make sacrifices if necessary, to give each child adequate preparation for this life's work. We were also trained to think learning important, and books, but "bad" books our mother burned. We valued music and art and craftsmanship but it was people and their welfare and religion that were the foci around which our lives seemed naturally to move. Above all else, the important thing was what we "planned to do with our lives." That each of us must do something was as inevitable as breathing for we owed a "debt to society which must be paid." This was a family commandment.

While many of our neighbors spent their energies in counting limbs on the family tree and grafting some on now and then to give symmetry to it, or in reliving the old bitter days of Reconstruction licking scars to cure their vague malaise, or in fighting each battle and turn of battle of that Civil War which has haunted the southern conscience so long, my father was pushing his nine children straight into the future. "You have your heritage," he used to say, "some of it good, some not so good; and as far as I know you had the usual number of grandmothers and grandfathers. Yes, there were slaves, far too many of them in the family, but that was your grandfather's mistake, not yours. The past has been lived. It is gone. The future is yours. What are you going to do with it?" Always he asked this question of his children, and sometimes one knew it was but an echo of the old question he had spent his life trying to answer for himself. For always the future held my father's dreams; always there, not in the past, did he expect to find what he had spent his life searching for.

We lived the same segregated life as did other southerners but our parents talked in excessively Christian and democratic terms. We were told ten thousand times that status and money are unimportant (though we were well supplied with both); we were told that "all men are brothers," that we are a part of a democracy and must act like democrats. We were told that the teachings of Jesus are real and important and could be practiced if we tried. We were told also that to be "radical" is bad, silly too; and that one must always conform to the "best behavior" of one's community and make it better if one can. We were taught that we were superior not to people but to hate and resentment, and that no member of the Smith family could stoop so low as to have an enemy. No matter what injury was done us, we must not injure ourselves further by retaliating. That was a family commandment too.

We had family prayers once each day. All of us as children read the Bible in its entirety each year. We memorized hundreds of Bible verses and repeated them at breakfast, and said "sentence prayers" around the family table. God was not someone we met on Sunday but a permanent member of our household. It never occurred to me until I was fourteen or fifteen years old that He did not see every act and thought and chalk up the daily score on eternity's tablets.

Despite the strain of living so intimately with God, the

nine of us were strong, healthy, energetic youngsters who filled our days with play and sports and music and books and managed to live much of our lives on the careless level at which young lives should be lived. We had our times of profound anxiety of course, for there were hard lessons to be learned about the body and "bad things" to be learned about sex. Sometimes I have wondered how we ever learned them with a mother so shy with words.

She was a wistful creature who loved beautiful things like lace and sunsets and flowers in a vague inarticulate way, and took good care of her children. We always knew this was not her world but one she accepted under duress. Her private world we rarely entered, though the shadow of it lay at times heavily on our hearts.

Our father owned large business interests, employed hundreds of colored and white laborers, paid them the prevailing low wages, worked them the prevailing long hours, built for them mill towns (Negro and white), built for each group a church, saw to it that religion was supplied free, saw to it that a commissary supplied commodities at a high price, and in general managed his affairs much as ten thousand other southern businessmen manage theirs.

Even now, I can hear him chuckling as he told my mother how he won his fight for Prohibition. The high point of the campaign was election afternoon, when he lined up the entire mill force of several hundred (white and black), passed out a shining silver dollar to each one of them, marched them in and voted liquor out of our county. It was a great day in his life. He had won the Big Game, a game he was always playing with himself against all kinds of evil. It did not occur to him to scrutinize the methods he used. Evil was a word written in capitals; the devil was smart; if you wanted to win you outsmarted him. It was as simple as that.

He was a practical, hardheaded, warmhearted, high-spirited man born during the Civil War, earning his living at twelve, struggling through bitter decades of Reconstruction and post-Reconstruction, through populist movement, through the panic of 1893, the panic of 1907, on into the twentieth century accepting his region as he found it, accepting its morals and its mores as he accepted its climate, with only scorn for those who held grudges against the North or pitied themselves or the South; scheming, dreaming, expanding his business, making and losing money, making friends whom he did not lose, with never a doubt that God was always by his side whispering hunches as to how to pull off successful deals. When he lost, it was his own fault. When he won, God had helped him.

Once while we were kneeling at family prayers the fire siren at the mill sounded the alarm that the mill was on fire. My father did not falter from his prayer. The alarm sounded again and again—which signified that the fire was big. With quiet dignity he continued his talk with God while his children sweated and wriggled and hearts beat out of their chests in excitement. He was talking to God—how could he hurry out of the presence of the Most High to save his mills! When he finished his prayer, he quietly stood up, laid the Bible carefully on the table. Then, and only then, did he show an interest in what was happening in Mill Town. . . . When the telegram was placed in his hands telling of the death of his beloved favorite son, he gathered his children together, knelt down, and in a steady voice which contained no hint of his shattered heart, loyally repeated, "God is our refuge and strength, a very present help in trouble. Therefore will we not fear, though the earth be removed, and

though the mountains be carried into the midst of the sea."
On his deathbed, he whispered to his old Business Partner
in Heaven: "I have fought the fight; I have kept the faith."

Against this backdrop the drama of the South was played
out one day in my life:

A little white girl was found in the colored section of our
town, living with a Negro family in a broken-down shack.
This family had moved in only a few weeks before and little
was known of them. One of the ladies in my mother's club,
while driving over to her washerwoman's, saw the child
swinging on a gate. The shack, as she said, was hardly more
than a pigsty and this white child was living with ignorant
and dirty and sick-looking colored folks. "They must have
kidnapped her," she told her friends. Genuinely shocked,
the clubwomen busied themselves in an attempt to do something, for the child was very white indeed. The strange
Negroes were subjected to a grueling questioning and finally
grew frightened and evasive and refused to talk at all. This
only increased the suspicion of the white group, and the
next day the clubwomen, escorted by the town marshal,
took the child from her adopted family despite their tears.

She was brought to our home. I do not know why my
mother consented to this plan. Perhaps because she loved
children and always showed tenderness and concern for
them. It was easy for one more to fit into our ample household and Janie was soon at home there. She roomed with
me, sat next to me at the table; I found Bible verses for her
to say at breakfast; she wore my clothes, played with my
dolls and followed me around from morning to night. She
was dazed by her new comforts and by the interesting activities of this big lively family; and I was as happily dazed,
for her adoration was a new thing to me; and as time passed

a quick, childish, and deepy felt bond grew up between us.

But a day came when a telephone message was received from a colored orphanage. There was a meeting at our home, whispers, shocked exclamations. All afternoon the ladies went in and out of our house talking to Mother in tones too low for children to hear. And as they passed us at play, most of them looked quickly at Janie and quickly looked away again, though a few stopped and stared at her as if they could not tear their eyes from her face. When my father came home in the evening Mother closed her door against our young ears and talked a long time with him. I heard him laugh, heard Mother say, "But Papa, this is no laughing matter!" And then they were back in the living room with us and my mother was pale and my father was saying, "Well, work it out, honey, as best you can. After all, now that you know, it is pretty simple."

In a little while my mother called my sister and me into her bedroom and told us that in the morning Janie would return to Colored Town. She said Janie was to have the dresses the ladies had given her and a few of my own, and the toys we had shared with her. She asked me if I would like to give Janie one of my dolls. She seemed hurried, though Janie was not to leave until next day. She said, "Why not select it now?" And in dreamlike stiffness I brought in my dolls and chose one for Janie. And then I found it possible to say, "Why? Why is she leaving? She likes us, she hardly knows them. She told me she had been with them only a month."

"Because," Mother said gently, "Janie is a little colored girl."

"But she can't be. She's white!"

"We were mistaken. She is colored."

"But she looks——"

"She is colored. Please don't argue!"

"What does it mean?" I whispered.

"It means," Mother said slowly, "that she has to live in Colored Town with colored people."

"But why? She lived here three weeks and she doesn't belong to them, she told me she didn't."

"She is a little colored girl."

"But you said yourself that she has nice manners. You said that," I persisted.

"Yes, she is a nice child. But a colored child cannot live in our home."

"Why?"

"You know, dear! You have always known that white and colored people do not live together."

"Can she come over to play?"

"No."

"I don't understand."

"I don't either," my young sister quavered.

"You're too young to understand. And don't ask me again, ever again, about this!" Mother's voice was sharp but her face was sad and there was no certainty left there. She hurried out and busied herself in the kitchen and I wandered through that room where I had been born, touching the old familiar things in it, looking at them, trying to find the answer to a question that moaned in my mind like a hurt thing. . . .

And then I went out to Janie, who was waiting, knowing things were happening that concerned her but waiting until they were spoken aloud.

I do not know quite how the words were said but I told her that she was to return in the morning to the little place where she had lived because she was colored and colored children could not live with white children.

"Are you white?" she said.

"I'm white," I replied, "and my sister is white. And you're colored. And white and colored can't live together because my mother says so."

"Why?" Janie whispered.

"Because they can't," I said. But I knew, though I said it firmly, that something was wrong. I knew my father and mother whom I passionately admired had done that which did not fit in with their teachings. I knew they had betrayed something which they held dear. And I was shamed by their failure and frightened, for I felt that they were no longer as powerful as I had thought. There was something Out There that was stronger than they and I could not bear to believe it. I could not confess that my father, who had always solved the family dilemmas easily and with laughter, could not solve this. I knew that my mother who was so good to children did not believe in her heart that she was being good to this child. There was not a word in my mind that said it but my body knew and my glands, and I was filled with anxiety.

But I felt compelled to believe they were right. It was the only way my world could be held together. And, like a slow poison, it began to seep through me: *I was white. She was colored. We must not be together. It was bad to be together. Though you ate with your nurse when you were little, it was bad to eat with any colored person after that. It was bad just as other things were bad that your mother had told you. It was bad that she was to sleep in the room with me that night. It was bad. . . .*

I was suddenly full of guilt. For three weeks I had done things that white children are not supposed to do. And now I knew these things had been wrong.

I went to the piano and began to play, as I had always

done when I was in trouble. I tried to play Paderewski's *Minuet* and as I stumbled through it, the little girl came over and sat on the bench with me. Feeling lonely, lost in these deep currents that were sweeping through our house that night, she crept closer and put her arms around me and I shrank away as if my body had been uncovered. I had not said a word, I did not say one, but she knew, and tears slowly rolled down her little white face. . . .

And then I forgot it. For more than thirty years the experience was wiped out of my memory. But that night, and the weeks it was tied to, worked its way like a splinter, bit by bit down to the hurt places in my memory and festered there. And as I grew older, as more experiences collected around that faithless time, as memories of earlier, more profound hurts crept closer and closer drawn to that night as if to a magnet, I began to know that people who talked of love and Christianity and democracy did not mean it. That is a hard thing for a child to learn. I still admired my parents, there was so much that was strong and vital and sane and good about them and I never forgot this; I stubbornly believed in their sincerity, as I do to this day, and I loved them. Yet in my heart they were under suspicion. Something was wrong.

Something was wrong with a world that tells you that love is good and people are important and then forces you to deny love and to humiliate people. I knew, though I would not for years confess it aloud, that in trying to shut the Negro race away from us, we have shut ourselves away from so many good, creative, honest, deeply human things in life. I began to understand so slowly at first but more and more clearly as the years passed, that the warped, distorted frame we have put around every Negro child from birth is around every white child also. Each is on a different side of the frame but each is pinioned there. And I knew that what cruelly shapes and cripples the personality of one is as cruelly shaping and crippling the personality of the other. I began to see that though we may, as we acquire new knowledge, live through new experiences, examine old memories, gain the strength to tear the frame from us, yet we are stunted and warped and in our lifetime cannot grow straight again any more than can a tree, put in a steel-like twisting frame when young, grow tall and straight when the frame is torn away at maturity.

As I sit here writing, I can almost touch that little town, so close is the memory of it. There it lies, its main street lined with great oaks, heavy with matted moss that swings softly even now as I remember. A little white town rimmed with Negroes, making a deep shadow on the whiteness. There it lies, broken in two by one strange idea. Minds broken in two. Hearts broken. Conscience torn from acts. A culture split in a thousand pieces. That is segregation. I am remembering: a woman in a mental hospital walking four steps out, four steps in, unable to go further because she has drawn an invisible line around her small world and is terrified to take one step beyond it. . . . A man in a Disturbed Ward assigning "places" to the other patients and violently insisting that each stay in his place. . . . A Negro woman saying to me so quietly, "We cannot ride together on the bus, you know. It is not legal to be human in Georgia."

Memory, walking the streets of one's childhood . . . of the town where one was born.

~ 2 ~

Custom and Conscience

THAT WAS long ago.

In the South, paint has peeled off of old houses we were born in; steps have sagged down. Foundations of economics and politics and old ways of living have crumbled though the rotted framework stands. The new has begun. Rows of brick cottages here and there shut out the sight of the old big houses and shanties. People have moved to town. There is more money. Tractors and bulldozers, cover crops and contour plowing have filled deep gullies and made green pastures of worn-out land. Factories are building in small-town vacant lots where we children played ball or in springtime picked yellow flycatchers from little damp places. Unions have their meetings in old second-story rooms where Woodmen of the World or the Red Men once held their weekly conclaves. Jukebox and hotdog stand, slot machine and tourist camp edge the black strip that has unrolled across clay and sand and swamp and hill.

How far away it seems now since that old horse-and-buggy clop clop of years made childhood so painful and wondrous a time of slow watching! Those old crowded years when eyes had time to look seem now as if they moved under a microscope.

On that dreary evening, when I wandered through our big house trying to fit good and evil into something that made sense, there was not one automobile in our town. Few people had heard of Kitty Hawk and the brothers who had learned to fly. I remember the day the first telephone came to our town. The night the first electric lights were turned on. The first flush toilet that was installed in my mother's bathroom.

During these forty years since I was a little girl struggling with conscience and custom, this old earth has seen more change in men's ways than in thousands of years of its history.

One keeps turning the pages. . . . In Europe, Sigmund Freud was already embattled by the fear and hatred of men who recognized too well the power of his findings, but we had not heard of him in the South or in most of America. No one had begun to worry about the hidden terror in the unconscious; no one apparently guessed that children had a sex life and that guilt is a crushing burden to lay on a baby's mind, though Stendhal had written his biography and Dostoievsky his novels and Rousseau his confessions and the old Greek plays had been acted thousands of times in the Western world. Insanity might be upstairs in the room whose door was always kept closed but no one talked of it and no one believed it could be otherwise. . . . Few knew the names of Einstein and Planck or had read the words *quantum theory,* and atomic energy was a vague daydream that men put in escape stories. Many in the rural South had not yet heard of Newton, and evolution was to most southern people not controversy but a sin that only infidels or those who believed in the "Higher Criticism" dared even read about.

In a corner of Austria the greatest murderer the world has ever known was living his childhood; Stalin was a young peasant in that beautiful old province on the Black Sea that has a name like ours; and the adolescent Kafka was beginning his terrifying trials that drove him, years later, to write down anxiety dreams that we shiveringly claim as our own now as we read them; Picasso had not learned yet to lay the thin slivers of a broken world in blocks of color so hypnotic with ugliness and strange truth that men can scarcely pull their eyes from the sight of it, though his culture had already shown him how, but was still dipping his brush in misty blues and dreaming of a whole person who no longer existed. In South Africa, Gandhi was weaving a way of change out of nonviolence and love and *satyagraha* which decades later would free four hundred million of his people in India. The Soongs were obscure Methodists whose best friends were missionaries; Chiang Kai-shek was a peasant boy in his teens riding the family's buffalo home in the evenings across rice paddies that lay shadowed by the mountains of Chekiang; and Franklin Roosevelt was a young college man spending carefree summers on the island of Campobello. Strangers one to another, distant and remote . . . yet all were being pulled inexorably together and we were pulled with them by men in laboratories, who wrapped their invisible theories around the old earth tighter and tighter and squeezed it into so small a thing that even now we cannot believe it.

Even yet, in the South, we still try to live as if none of this has happened. The old signs are still over the minds of men. Custom and conscience still divide our children and southern tradition is a ghost that everybody still believes in.

I saw a group of southern children try their strength against that ghost a few summers ago. It happened on our mountain where the children were spending the summer. We were gathered in the big gymnasium-theater making a play. It was the children's affair and was concerned with Every Child who makes a journey through the universe to collect new experiences which he needs in order to grow up. They had read Antoine de Saint Exupéry's fantasy *The Little Prince* and, borrowing from it, had agreed that in their play Every Child was born on a planet, too, where no one lives but himself but if he grows, he does not stay there. There are other planets which he must visit. In such simple pictures they saw the old troubled story of man's progress. A camper was chosen for the role of Every Child and given the name the Prince. The first planet to be visited on this journey was Your Own Family. The Prince's first traveling companion joined him here and the campers named her Conscience, made her into a tall nursemaid, prissy and prudish, and designed a bristling costume for her that contained surely all the angularities of their combined early experiences.

The Prince had begun his journey. The second experience was concerned with the weaning from the nipple to the cup. There were many others: the first day at school, getting rid of one's fear of the dark, making a friend, creating things with one's hands. As the play grew, the children realized that the Prince must have more traveling companions—Conscience did not seem adequate for so hazardous a journey. So Southern Tradition was chosen as his second companion, and a group of eight dancers were selected who were to stay close to the Prince, blocking his way or opening it, as he traveled. The third companion they chose was Religion. "I know we should take religion along," one child said, "but it just doesn't seem to belong on the stage with the others—after all, it's near us only on Sundays."

"Then put it in the balcony," another called out. And they

did, asking five girls to take their Bibles with them to the far balcony and sit there.

The fourth companion chosen was Science—though it was not an easy thing to convince the group that the Prince needed this traveling companion. But Science had one ardent defendant in a quiet, withdrawn girl who rarely took part in discussions. Now she spoke up. "We live in the age of science," she said. "And we shouldn't make a journey through the universe with only a nursemaid like Conscience, and Southern Tradition and Religion. It's too dangerous. There are times when the Prince better know some facts."

"Yes, but about what? He can't take things like refrigerators with him on a journey through the universe!"

"Things aren't science," the quiet camper replied. "Science makes things, but science," she groped for words, "is really the search for truth. It's not easy to find truth, for you must test it and test it. The Prince may need the truth if he gets far from home. I think it would be bad not to take science along to help him find it."

Science was reluctantly chosen and put on the other balcony opposite religion. The Prince continued his journey.

Now we were in trouble. The Prince had spoken new words. She said, "I was born on a planet where I live all alone. I have journeyed to other planets and have had strange and wonderful experiences. I have lived with my family. I have gone to school. I have felt lonely and I have failed. But I am no longer afraid of the dark and there are things I know that once I did not know. I have made things with my hands. I have also made a friend and that was nice and I shall never forget it. I have had a date. I have family memories that are good and some I hate to remember and all of them I take with me wherever I journey."

She looked up quickly at the campers and counselors who were watching the play grow. "Last night," she continued, "I thought, Here we are making a play about visiting planets and have forgot that we live on a planet called Earth. It is a star hanging in the sky and must seem a pretty thing to the rest of the universe but I haven't traveled far on it and I don't know anything much about its people. Most of it is cut off from me and part of my town is cut off, too. We are children living on the earth and I think to grow up we should play with all the earth's children. That is an important experience, which the Prince in our play has never had. Don't you think he should have it?"

For a long moment no one answered. Then a youngster burst out, "Yes, but you know we can't play with all children! It will ruin our play if we try. We can't have a happy ending if we do that."

Voices were angry now as one after another had something to say. "You know this. Why did you mention it?"

"Why can't we end it with a nice experience that isn't controversial?"

"Yes, something we can really do!"

"After all, why bring up things——"

The little Prince said, "But this journey through the universe means having experiences that will make children mature. We've talked about it for three or four summers. The Prince can't be emotionally mature if he refuses to play with other children, you know that. We decided that last summer. He's got to be interested in everybody. The earth is every child's home. What's the sense of the Prince's making this journey if he doesn't meet all kinds of people? Is he going to see just white people like us here at camp? He might as well sit at home if that's all he's going to do."

"Then for goodness sakes, let him play with the Chinese or somebody safe!"

"It wouldn't be honest! If he plays with children he must play with children in Mill Town and colored children too, right here in Georgia."

"Oh my goodness! Then we can't. And you know it. Why be so silly!"

"Down here we just can't——"

"Daddy says——"

"My mother says——"

The old battle of words was on and the accent was very southern. The gong sounded for lunch. Quiet Hour came. Then swimming, tennis, other activities. It was not until next day that we returned to the play. When the group was seated, I suggested that we talk about it as people who honestly want to grow up to be mature, and who know you don't give up something you want just because things get hard. "Yesterday, everybody was excited. Today, well, let's see what the four traveling companions can suggest. After all, that's what they're for, isn't it?

The actors had made their own lines from the beginning of the play. Now one of them said, "Shall we make our words or will you help us? You know, since this is a kind of emergency."

"Make your own lines. As honestly as you know how."

The Prince's eyes were bright as she stepped out to the center of the stage. "I am an earth child," she said proudly. "And this is a planet I live on. I would like to play with all its children for I, too, am its child."

The children who were not in the play sat on the floor, watching. On the stage were Conscience the nursemaid and the eight girls who were Southern Tradition. On the two balconies were Religion and Science. Both balcony groups had come to the play-making with armfuls of books, to meet this emergency.

"I think," a child from the floor spoke, "that we can still get out of this mess if Conscience will only tell the Prince that we can't play with other children because we don't know their games."

"But we do," the Prince said quickly. "All children play with balls and chase each other. If they don't, they can learn in five minutes. Anyway, that's a tricky way out and I won't use it." She turned quickly to Conscience. "Conscience, will you let me play with the colored children here at home?" In an aside to us, "We might as well get to the point, don't you think?"

Conscience ad-libbed her lines. "Don't be silly," she replied calmly. "When race is the issue I always refer you to Southern Tradition. You know that. Why don't you ask her?" Southern Tradition's eight girls blocked the Prince's path. "This is our answer," their leader said. "If you try it, we will hurt you."

The Prince's cheeks flushed up. A little seven-year-old covered her eyes. Each camper in that room was living this play now as if it were her own biography.

The Prince turned to me, "What next?"

"You have other resources. See what Religion says."

The girls in Religion's balcony were ready. They read in chorus a part of the Sermon on the Mount. They read, "For God so loved the world, that He gave His only begotten Son. . . ." And then one girl said clearly and with such deep simplicity that it was truly moving, "Suffer little children to come unto me, and forbid them not: for of such is the kingdom of God."

"Conscience, did you hear?"

Conscience turned away arrogantly, "I never listen to Religion where segregation is involved. No one does, down here."

Even as Conscience answered, the eight who were Southern Tradition had quickly encircled the Prince and now were forcing her back from her journey toward the earth children.

"I think," a youngster called out from among those watching, "that Religion is no good as a traveling companion as long as it stays up in the balcony. Why doesn't Religion come down here and push Custom back where it belongs?"

"But Religion doesn't do that in the South," a girl from the balcony answered. "Religion stays out of controversies. You know that. Our place is up here."

"How about Science?" I asked.

The five who were Science had their answers and gave them, quoting Ruth Benedict and Margaret Meade and others on culture and race, but even as they talked, Conscience turned away in great boredom. "I can't hear Science's words. The only thing that Science is good for, I think, is to make things like bombs and planes. Anyway, this isn't my affair. It is Southern Tradition's."

"You haven't a chance," a nine-year-old camper called out to the Prince in great excitement. "Religion's 'way off on her balcony, reading the Bible. Science is 'way off on its balcony, making things and writing books. They're not worth a thing as traveling companions! You may as well give up. Southern Tradition is too strong."

But suddenly the Prince had begun to run. She twisted and turned, ran quickly, ran slowly; yet always the eight who were Southern Tradition blocked her way. She had lost herself in her struggle, long ago had stopped acting, and finally I called to her to stop, fearing that she would exhaust herself. She fell on the floor, breathing hard, and lay there, staring up at the ceiling.

I can never forget that moment as I looked at those children. They sat so still, a hundred campers and counselors, looking at something they had never seen before. And I sat there, remembering a day long ago that I had almost forgotten.

"The little Prince can never grow up," one said softly.

"Maybe we shouldn't have tried. Maybe it would have been better if the little Prince had stayed in Saint Exupéry's book."

"Oh, I knew yesterday something bad was about to happen! Why did the Prince feel that we must play with all the earth's children? You knew we couldn't do it!"

"Because," the Prince answered, doggedly, "the Prince in our play wants to be mature. We know here at camp that it is right to feel this way. *Our* conscience has changed whether the one in the play has or not. There should be a way to work it out. Religion and Science should have helped me; I wasn't strong enough to do it by myself."

"But they couldn't—honestly! This is the way the traveling companions are in the South. This is the way Conscience is too. We can't pretend a lie," Conscience hotly defended herself and the others.

The play had to be mended. I told them that things were as their actors had said but things need not be that way. A day would come soon when the little Prince could play with the earth's children. Therefore it seemed to me that we might bridge over the gap in time. We could let Religion come down from the balcony and help. But I felt we must decide first what religion is. Is it reading the Bible and singing hymns and being Protestant or Catholic or Jew or Christian Scientist, or is it something more important?

Everyone was again talking, eager to find a way out of this impasse which they themselves had created. Religion is love, an older girl said, for no human mind has dreamed of anything better than love, so it must be love. "Yes, it is love," the little ones chimed in, relieved that the talk was growing more pleasant. Love, they continued, can help push Southern Tradition off the stage and teach it a few lessons about being nice to other people if Science will come down from its balcony to help.

Quickly the young scientists came down and joined the Prince and quickly they improvised a dance in which they drove Southern Tradition—nonviolently of course!—into the wings of the stage, then they turned on Conscience. They told her she was a coward always to be listening to Southern Tradition: why couldn't she grow up and learn things from Religion and Science! And then as quickly, the campers watching this, decided that they could impersonate earth children, they could *be* Chinese and Japanese and Germans and Russians and Negroes, they could come from the ends of the earth and play with the little Prince. And they did this. Then a counselor put Beethoven's Seventh Symphony on the recording machine and the old gymnasium where we had played and worked for twenty-five summers filled with sounds of triumph as we made a great circle and danced together in earth-unison.

It was make-believe and we knew it. But we could not let our play die as so much that is young has died on that old wall, segregation. But at supper, the children looked tired and preoccupied and I knew we had failed to answer the question twisting in their minds.

Late that evening, long after the lights in the cabins were out, a camper came into my office. She was an older girl who had spent many summers on the mountain, now ready for college in the fall. She stood there a moment pale and tense, and then began to talk. I did not record that conversation but it has fixed itself in my mind so deeply that I do not think I shall distort its truth as I put it down here.

"I don't know how to begin; I shock myself as I try," she faltered and then the words rushed from her, "I think you have done a terrible thing to children."

"Tell me why you think so."

"You see," she was sorting the words that had piled up during her sleeplessness, "you have made us want to be good. *Mature*, you've called it. You taught us to be honest, not to cover up things. You made us think it fine to be like that, even when it hurt. All these years, you've said so much about human dignity—it's a nice phrase. . . ." She went to the window and looked out on the old peak beyond the tennis courts.

"But it's all wrong!" She turned back quickly. "You made us think of ourselves as no better than other people. You shouldn't have done that. Oh, I can't find my words, the feelings are too close here," she touched her throat.

"Perhaps you would like to wait and tell me tomorrow."

"No. I'd lose my nerve by morning. You told us we were like all children everywhere; that money and color, the church you go to, don't make any difference. And the kids here believed you. You said the only real differences have to do with values and interests and tastes. And you said that the most precious right a human has is his right to be different. Even his right to be dull." She smiled suddenly. "We liked that. And we believed you. We loved you for giving us ideals that we could be proud of. We wanted to live them. They seemed so fine." She laughed a bitter little laugh, then added softly, "But I almost hate you tonight, for letting us fall in love with beliefs that I see now we can't possibly live. Why did you teach us to want to be mature when you knew there was no place down here for such people?

"When I go back to my town, how can I live these ideals! Tell me, if you can—oh, but you can't! That's what I have just realized.

"I saw it today as we worked on the play. For the first time in my life! I guess you've tried to tell us but somehow I didn't see it. It always seemed something we could do—when we were grown. Well, I see now. And I think the others saw it too, though most are too young to find words for their feelings. Maybe they're lucky."

She came close to my desk. "It was as if somebody had swung a bright mirror in front of us. The whole thing opened up in that moment! How it would be—if we tried to live the way we have learned to want to live. Can't you imagine my town—if I were to go home and invite a colored girl to Sunday school? Or even try to get one of the girls in Mill Town in my sorority? They'd think I was crazy. Suppose I said to a colored girl, 'Let's go in the drugstore and have a coke'? Can't you see their faces—Mother's and Daddy's—and everybody's! Well, I can—especially if they arrested me and put me in jail.

"I'd be breaking a law, wouldn't I, if I tried to live these ideals in my home town?"

"Yes. You would be breaking a law."

"Do you think we should break laws? Do you *want* us to be lawbreakers? Oh, I know! I even know I could break the law and they wouldn't dare put me in jail, because of Daddy. But that only makes it worse, for they would put others there. We forgot to take law along as a traveling companion, didn't we? Maybe it's better. It might make the little ones wonder if *anybody* has any sense down here.

"I'm saying these things because I'm scared—at what I am looking at in me."

She said no more for a little and I did not try to talk.

"Who put those signs over doors?" she asked suddenly. "Somebody must keep them there. Is it my father? He owns a textile mill and hates the FEPC. No, don't tell me. I don't want to know if he has anything to do with it—I couldn't believe it—he's so good—I've never seen Daddy do an unkind thing in all my life. Sometimes Mother loses her temper. Not Daddy. Then *why* does he want to keep Negroes segregated —what pleasure does he get out of it? Does it make him richer to keep them that way?"

"Some people think so."

"But why does he care that much for money? Why would he be willing to——" She said no more for what seemed a long time. I was searching hard for the right answer to give her.

She said more quietly, "Mother reads the *Nation* and the *New Republic*. All those papers. I wonder why. . . . If they've made up their minds that the signs stay up and segregation is going to be here forever, then why do they fool themselves? Why don't they be honest about it? Why pretend and go to church and say nice words? It doesn't make sense! What does religion mean to them? If it isn't real, what do they get out of it?

"I've been here six summers. I've grown to love this old mountain . . . the courtesy every one shows children; the dignity they bestow on the little ones. It's nice. We laugh so much here. . . . I've learned to paint and my drive has improved in tennis; I can even dance, a little. And the idea of growing—I've liked that. The way we've learned to think our bodies are honorable. No shame. . . . I remember you said freedom and responsibility are like Siamese twins: they die if they are cut apart. . . . All these things. . . . No punishment . . . just understanding . . . reaching out to accept other people as human beings like ourselves. We've all said we were going to bring up our children that way.

"I remember when we learned about hate. I was so afraid of that word—I used to deny that I hated anyone. And then, one day, you told us that human relationships are what the personality is fed on: love is the part you grow on, hate the part you don't need, the waste that is excreted. You said our job is to find sanitary ways of getting rid of it so it won't harm others, or ourselves. That was such a relief, to know that hate is as natural as a bowel movement and much the same thing. I stopped biting my nails when I learned that." She smiled and looked down at her hands. "I remember so well those Sunday mornings when we've discussed these things, sitting under the trees."

I said, "You think it's wrong—what we have learned here together?"

"I think it's useless. It just tears us up inside! Makes us so raw. Oh, I hate to say it, but I do think you have harmed us. You've unfitted us for the South. And yet, this is where we shall live. Unless we run away.

"I think you should have made it easier for us to live here. What is education for if not that! Since we have to practice segregation, why didn't you make us think it is right?"

"How could it be right?"

"Oh, I don't know! I'm all confused. My mind feels as if it is full of barbed wire. It isn't right for any one to feel the way I feel—inside.

"When I have children, I am not going to give them a single ideal they can't practice. I don't want them torn up like this. I'll tell them that Jim Crow is fine, that it's legal, that this is the way things are in the South and the way they are going to stay. I'll tell them they have the right to push folks around; that they *should* decide where their inferiors can sit and stand and what doors they can go through. That it's right to shame colored children by making them go through back doors and behind curtains—"

She came to my desk. "I haven't told you about last winter. Daddy took me to New York—we were in the dining car— had just finished our soup—when I saw the steward seat the president of that college in Atlanta behind those curtains. I had heard him make a speech at a church meeting. I said, 'Daddy, did you see that? He's the president of a college!' And Daddy said, 'That's where colored folks are supposed to sit. You mustn't get silly notions, honey.' I couldn't finish my dinner. I know it was morbid, but I kept looking at all those faces wondering why they felt they had to have a curtain between them and the president of a college, just to eat their dinner. And it began to seem so crazy!

"I'll teach my children not to *think* about things like this. I'll teach them that money comes first, before people, that it's more important. I won't let them be hypocrites, like me."

"In other words, you would make little Nazis out of them."

"At least it would be honest!"

"I'm afraid honesty doesn't have much to do with it, though it would be logical. Your feelings have stampeded a little, haven't they?"

"I'm scared," she whispered. "I don't like the future. It doesn't seem to belong to us. It's as if older people have stolen it from us. I don't know what to believe about anything. I'm seventeen years old and I have no idea what is wrong and what is right—not enough to know how to live. And even if I knew, I couldn't live it down here. I lay there tonight try- ing to tell myself that segregation is right. I said it over and

over as I used to do as a child when I was memorizing. I said
'Daddy knows more than we know here at camp. There's no
sense in worrying about it.' But it didn't help.

"You see," her voice had quieted, "I want so much to go
home and be decent about things. Not make folks mad—just
live what I believe is right. But how? Tell me how! What
shall I do when I get on a bus—go to the front with the white
folks? Or shall I speak to the motorman and make a little
scene each time I get on? Shall I keep on going through
White doors? Can I persuade my class to invite a colored
girl to Sunday school? Suppose I get that far—will the minister let me? I don't think he would—he would say, 'These
things have to come slowly, my dear,' and he would mean
that they must not come at all, as long as there is any risk in
it. If I do these things that seem so important to us up here,
everybody at home will be furious. I can't take it."

"What are you afraid of?"

"I don't know. It's like waking up in the night after a
dream—you're just scared, you don't know why. I just can't
fight people I love. Maybe it's because I want to be liked too
much. But it's right to want people to like you, isn't it?"

"Yes," I was feeling old, "it's right to want people to like
you."

"Funny," she said, "I don't want to hate and I don't want
people to hate me. That ought to be a good way to feel. But
you won't change things down here if you feel that way. Do
you remember the book you gave me to read on the well-
adjusted child? Well, that's me—I'm beginning to see it. I'm
just too easygoing. To change things you've got to get mad
when you see folks do what you think is wrong. But I can't
stand people who shout and scream and push others around
in the name of good. They seem crazy. And I don't want anybody calling *me* a crackpot—that's what Daddy calls people.

"It makes you feel very tired inside to think things like this," she turned away to hide her tears.

I said, "I would like for you to let me talk a little now. And I have to begin before you were born."

And then I told her what I have written down here.

✧ 3 ✧

Unto the Third and Fourth Generation

"YOU HAVE to remember," I said, "that much of the trouble we are in started long ago. Your parents didn't make it, nor I. We were born into it. Signs were put over doors when we were babies. We took them for granted just as we took heat and sandspurs and mosquitoes. We worried about things close home but I don't think we noticed the signs. Somehow we seemed always to walk through the right door. People find it hard to question something that has been here since they were born.

"Before these signs went up, there had been a bad war in which people were killed, homes burned that held all of a family's memories. That isn't an easy thing to forget. Before that war, there had been a way of living that destroyed human dignity, and for a long time people in the South did not even think those words. These were evil experiences for white and Negro, rich and poor, but they were curiously complicated by the attitude of the North and South toward each other.

"Perhaps the best way to explain that attitude is to think of two brothers, each of whom is 'on the make,' each of whom is greedy, sometimes ruthless in his determination to make money. But one makes his money easily, having figured a way to let others do it for him, and spends it lavishly on a gracious, luxurious life for his family; and having more leisure, he becomes more urbane, and 'charming' and his life more and more gay and pleasant, and without toil, while his wife is surrounded by servants who do everything for her. The other brother is industrious, his wife does the housework, he saves more, invests it shrewdly, considers himself more provident and 'sensible' than his brother but all the time he secretly envies his brother's sins for they seem more fun than his own and he covets his dominant power in the family's affairs. Feeling this way, he begins to think a great deal about his brother's sins. Especially does the fact bother him that his brother doesn't pay wages to his laborers. Although he does not pay much himself, he at least pays a little. And this makes him feel self-righteous. At the same time, he feels that his morals handicap him.

"Then things change. Machines are invented. The industrious brother, keeping wages down to almost a starvation level, begins to make money by building factories. As he gains in wealth and power, his brother on the farm finds it less easy to make a living even with slave labor. Each now begins to fight the other, for each wants to hold the balance of power in the family. Each insists that his way of making a living is best and even tries to force his way on the rest of the family.

"The brother who has made money so easily with slave labor watches his income dwindle year after year as compared to his brother's income which is doubling and quadrupling as more factories are built, and in his frustration, he declares that he is going to withdraw from the family unless his brother stops criticising him. The hardworking brother, still jealous, and just as greedy as the brother he has criticised so long, is shocked and declares that nothing can break up a family; no generation, however sharp its differences, has the right to tear a family to pieces. The argument shifts now and is concerned with this 'right' to withdraw and feelings grow more bitter. It is not long, with tempers so hot, before the two brothers are in terrible conflict and the rest of the family is forced to take sides with one or the other.

"Such feelings as these between North and South, make it impossible, even today, to say in a few words what the Civil War was about. It was about greed, and two systems that could not exist in the same country, and a lust for political power. It had to do also with a region's right to withdraw when it has quarreled with the rest of the nation. But regardless of *states' rights* and *union,* and competing economic systems, and the struggle for power in Congress, the war would not have been fought had there not been slavery.

"In the North, there was throughout these decades of conflict, a group of honest, thoughtful men and women who sincerely loved human freedom, who knew slavery would destroy the integrity not only of our democratic institutions but of our Christian people, whose hearts were stirred by the cruelties of the slave system in the South, and who spoke out at this time solely because of their concern for the Negro and his human rights. These were the abolitionists, a courageous, fine group of idealists whose words sprang from deep beliefs. The part of the North that was fighting for political power unscrupulously exploited them, using their fine honest words as a weapon to wage a holy war against the South by arousing the conscience of idealists at the same time that they stirred the patriotism of others over the threatened partition of their country.

"Our South understood too well these motives and was shaken by a terrible anger. The North's moral arguments were so obviously right; its desires so profoundly selfish. Southerners responded by as wild and arrogant and angry a defense as a hotheaded people could give. It is only by trying to understand these mixed feelings made of ideals and greed and power-lust and patriotism and regional jealousy that we can understand the feelings which, even today, the South has toward the North and many northerners have toward the South. There is still so much self-righteousness in the North and still so much hatred of the 'damyankee' in the South.

"Then the war came. And the South lost everything it cherished. And for a little while there was no room for hate in most men's hearts, for there was so much sadness. The whole region mourned its dead, its loss, its deep hurt. Sometimes it was the little things that were hardest to bear: a broken old tree under which one had played in childhood, charred camellias and boxwoods. . . . The ruins were so vast that only by finding a small loss to hover over could the human heart endure its emptiness. A heavy melancholy fell on minds and was never lifted from some of them. And then the terrible, the unforeseen happened: President Lincoln was killed by a southerner. A neurotic, unstable actor was the murderer but he was southern. The North's feelings that day and the next and the next were just what our country's would have been had a German assassinated Roosevelt—or what the South's would have been in those days had a northerner killed Lee.

"After Lincoln's tragic death, northern pulpits and press lost all objectivity and in righteous wrath demanded that the whole South be punished for this crime. Now once again the North was condemning us. They called the South a Problem, they called its people 'barbarians,' they insisted again and again that this proud people must be humbled. They blamed us for the terrible Reconstruction which followed; they blamed us for their own lack of planning and vision; they blamed us for the failures of their Freedmen's Bureau— which in spite of its muddle-headed seven years of existence still did a good and terribly needed job of helping more than four million ex-slaves find a life as freedmen. They hung our racial sins up for the world to look at, and at the same time began to practice these sins, under cover, up North. They blamed and grew rich and smug, and we hated and grew poor and stubborn.

"Hypocrisy, greed, self-righteousnes, defensiveness twisted and turned in men's minds. The South grew more and more sensitive to criticism, more and more defensive and dishonest in its own thinking. For deep down in their hearts, southerners knew they were wrong. They knew it in slavery just as they later knew that sharecropping was wrong, and as they know today that segregation is wrong. It was not only the North's criticism that made them defensive, it was their own conscience. Our grandparents called themselves Christians and sometimes believed they were. Believing it, they were compelled to believe that it was morally right for them to hold slaves. They could not say, 'We shall keep our slaves because they are profitable, regardless of right and wrong.' A few tough old realists who didn't claim to be in the Fold probably did say it. But to most, to say such words would have seemed as fantastic as a confession of their mixed reasons for opposing slavery would have seemed to the Yankees. Our grandfathers' conscience compelled them to justify slavery and they did: by making the black man 'different,' setting him outside God's law, reducing him to less than human. In a way that would have seemed blasphemous to them, had they stopped to think, they took God's place and 'decided' which of His creatures have souls and which do not. And once doing it, they continued doing it, and their sons continued doing it, and their grandsons, telling themselves and their children more and more and more lies about white superiority until they no longer knew the truth and were lost in a maze of fantasy and falsehood that had little resemblance to the actual world they lived in.

"It's a strange thing how a man's own conscience can trap his soul. But North and South, this happened to our people.

"But all the lies and defenses and fabulous justifications did not keep our people from feeling guilty; and feeling it, they felt also a need to suffer, and like guilty people everywhere, they had to find 'enemies' to be punished by. The 'damyankee' was the perfect psychological enemy, for had not this Yankee unjustly blamed the South for a sin which he too had committed in another form! And had not this Yankee 'unjustly punished' the whole South for this sin! And was not this Yankee even today 'persecuting' the South!

"The North felt guilty, also, for its greed and its hypocritical lying and the damage that had been done to the South. And feeling guilty, had to continue its criticisms of our region to justify itself. So it went. . . . And so it is today.

"The North and South were not a right and wrong cause fighting each other but two bad consciences, each covering up its guilt and its greed, each insisting on its right to sin in its own way, each having economic and religious and psychological reasons for doing so.

"And yet, back of this conflict waged by two bad consciences, was the Negro; back of it, was the terrible need of enslaved human beings to be free; but there were few, North or South, willing to face up to this problem. They were so concerned with themselves, with their hostility toward each other, and their hurt pride and hurt greed, that there was no room left in their minds and hearts for a concern for another group's rights. *Human rights, man's freedom. . . .* Such phrases were as remote as is the moon on a blazing hot day to these white men stricken by their burning hatred for each other.

"Most of our families could not take these traumatic experiences in a sane, creative way. There was too much. And their past life, their image ideals, their beliefs, their mental habits had not prepared them for this kind of trouble. Insight was not a quality their culture valued; nor intellectual honesty; nor self-criticism; nor concern for human rights; nor could they laugh at themselves. With all their capacity for gaiety and wit, they had so little real humor—it was the backwoodsman who possessed humor and his voice was not heard at this time. All these planter families had was courage and anger, and this was not enough.

"Yet there were many individuals, all over the South, who kept themselves without hate, admitting the South's mistakes, and refusing to believe in the tenets of white supremacy. There were others who showed great valor and personal courage in working out their own family problems, though they were defensive and confused in their thinking about their region. But most gave up, did things the easy way regardless of human consequences, thought the easy way, and identifying with the group, dissolved their own scruples by substituting for a personal conscience and a clear brain this thing our politicians call 'loyalty to southern tradition.'

"Event after hard event piled up on these people. The South was in chaos. Many had lost their citizenship, their homes, their possessions, and were psychological aliens in their own beloved country. And suddenly four million Negroes were 'freed' with nowhere to go, nowhere to sleep, no work, no food, no 'place,' no schools.

"And the Yankee accent was everywhere. Southerners began to hate the sound of it for so rarely did it come from mouths that spoke words of tact or sympathy. But, as miserable as was the whites' condition, and it was bad, the condition of Negroes was worse. It was this problem of rehabilitation of Negroes (the whites were left to shift for themselves) that the Freedmen's Bureau worked on. After all, though Congress found it hard to remember, the war had been fought to 'free the slaves.' The Bureau's blunders were a thing of horror, but at the same time, it did much that was urgently needed and that helped ease the worst strains. The Bureau found work for Negroes, negotiated labor contracts with white employers, opened schools for them and gave them much needed health care. But the white South now was too confused to feel relief that part of their region's burden was lifted in this way. Instead they hated these 'carpetbaggers' for their concern for Negroes and their lack of concern for whites. Like a jealous, sick, miserable child, they wanted everything done for them and had no capacity for pity for those worse off than themselves.

"But there were other northerners, not interested in Negroes, who came also, and stayed long after the Bureau closed up. And southerners worked side by side with them as they set up factories at the level of the South's starvation wages, and in this way, an odd kind of unity was finally established between the two regions. The North furnished the money, the South furnished the labor and the managerial talent and its region's resources, and it worked—as colonial systems always work, for a time.

"It worked for a time because these men, southern and

northern, had energy, when most of our families felt par-
alyzed by so much trouble. They knew things to do; they
went about doing them. They were often—southern and
northern—tough and selfish and greedy, but they brought
order out of chaos.

"In the rural regions, fewer northerners were seen, but
other southerners brought order there and that order was
based on the sharecropping system. No one stopped to examine its moral roots or its economic implications. People
needed a roof over their heads. They needed corn bread for
supper. Whites and Negroes took it when it was offered
them. They hungered for peace and a few quiet nights and
the knowledge that tomorrow they would have a little to eat,
and they were willing to pay any price for these necessities.

"In a way, sharecropping seemed a perfect solution. There
were few jobs available off the farms. Few factories, and few
men trained to do anything but farm work, and no money to
pay wages with. Confederate money was nothing but paper
after Lee surrendered. In our house, when I was a child,
there were piles of it in an old trunk upstairs. I remember we
children once took a basketful downtown to see if it would
buy a dime's worth of candy. When the storekeeper said,
'No,' my brother tried to bargain with him. 'Even a trunkful
of it?' he said. 'Not even a warehouse full,' the man answered.
We were stunned. But our grandfathers had no such illusions.
They knew they had nothing but land. So it seemed a good
thing to say: 'Now listen, you go back on the farm and get to
work. I'll feed you and you can live in one of the cabins.
When it's cotton-picking time, I'll pay you a share of what
you've raised on my land.' So the system began.

"But once beginning, there was no end to it. It made too
much money for a few folks, and too little for the rest for

them to ever buy land of their own, or ever leave to learn new trades or find new jobs. And it was so easy for the few. You sat in the big house and a hundred, maybe a thousand, colored and white folks raised your crop. Now and then, you put fertilizer on the land if you had the cash to buy it, or if you didn't you let them bleed it to death. You bought the seed, furnished a few mules, sat back and let the 'hands' do the rest. When fall came, you sold the cotton—or the tobacco— gave them their share or a part of it, depending on how honest you were. To feed the workers through the winter, you put up a commissary on your place, charged the colored and white folks high interest on the food you sold them 'on time' and deducted it in September when cotton was picked and weighed up. You, on the other hand, paid high interest at the bank for the money to carry your workers through the winter; you lost your crop sometimes when growing conditions were bad; prices were so low some years that you didn't make a cent and when that happened you had to feed the families on your place no matter how hard it was to do so; but the good years were good and when they came a few made fabulous profits. And these few dug in: buying the farms of their neighbors who were not as shrewd traders in the market as they, growing richer and more powerful as the years went by, controlling more and more sharecroppers, white and colored, who were as tied to these farms by low wages and long hours and ignorance as if they had been legal slaves.

"That is the way it began.

"My parents grew up in those troubled years and when we were born they tried to give us a better childhood than theirs had been. That meant material things but it meant ideals and values too. They gave us ideals that they did not practice and did not expect us to practice and that we could not practice when we wanted to. And yet they urged us to believe in them, though at the same time we were urged to believe in segregation too and loyalty to southern tradition.

"And that is what you find so hard to understand. And I too have found it hard. We have to remember the chaos, the confusion, the hurt feelings, the poverty. The church, that might have been a guiding principle through this bleak and terrifying time, had made so grave a compromise with Christian belief on the issue of slavery that its leaders, still defensive and guilty, were hardly in a position to give moral guidance. So, a kind of gentleman's agreement came about that a state of emergency existed within the areas of race and money and politics which necessitated a suspension of morals in these fields. Preachers, politicians, judges, planters, factory owners, and plain working folks agreed. People did not confess it aloud. They still talked about sin, and sometimes even about democracy. And as time went on, the less they practiced their ideals the more they cherished them, as if the ideals were something rare that was no longer durable enough for the life everybody had to live yet must be kept safe somewhere, at least in the corner of one's memory, and maybe some day could be lived again.

"Our people were meeting trouble by closing up their lives, their minds, their hearts, their consciences, trying not to see, not to feel things as they really were.

"When your parents and I were children, economic order had in a sense been restored although there was great poverty. But race feeling in the South had reached its peak. The decade before we were born, a thousand Negroes were lynched. The Klan had ridden in almost every county, drawing under its hood the haters and the hotheads from many families. People were terrified not only of Negroes but of their own capacity for cruelty, and panic-stricken at the lack of wise leadership. And in church, not a word was preached about these matters, no insight given that might have restrained excesses, no words said to encourage men and women to try to meet their challenge as Christian citizens living in a democracy.

"I have sometimes thought: Had there been a few men in the South with enough strength to be humble and admit their region's mistakes, with enough integrity and energy to act out their own beliefs and with a strong belief in freedom and a clear vision of a new way of life, our people might have been swung around with their faces turned to the future. But we had no leaders of moral and intellectual stature, no one of the quality of a Nehru in India; certainly no one comparable to Gandhi. We had only one Robert E. Lee, and he retired during the troubled times of Reconstruction to a college campus. There was Henry Grady, it is true, the 'conciliator,' who talked a certain kind of good common sense that seemed lucid and statesmanlike in comparison with most, though he showed little awareness of the profound problems of human rights so completely unsolved or of the economic and social needs of the eighty per cent of the whites who were not in the dominant group.

"But our leaders were, for the most part, hotheaded, immature, defensive, often greedy men, unwilling to accept criticism. Or else they were so tortured and ambivalent that they found it impossible to make important decisions quickly enough. So the South walked backward into its future. It is no wonder people were hurt on the journey.

"My oldest brother was born the year that the Supreme Court nullified the restrictive features of the Civil Rights Acts. And from then on the South felt that it was free to do what it wished about segregation. The first statutes were so profitable to politician and economic exploiter that more and more statutes were added. It happened so quickly that people did not realize what had been done to their lives.

"When we look back on those years, it seems as if the whole white South suffered a kind of moral breakdown. And yet, we must remember that there were no massive sadistic orgies as in Germany, no gas chambers, concentration camps, no Buchenwald and Dachau. Always the South's conscience hurt; always there were doubts and scruples; always hate was tempered with a little love, and always folks were inconsistent—which was a blessed thing for our region. Ideals seemed to be dead but at least their ghosts haunted men's souls.

"But in those eighty years after the Civil War nearly five thousand human beings *were* lynched. We can't forget that either, for it is a heavy sin for a democratic Christian people to live with. Yet it is different in quantity and quality from the six million Jews killed so quickly in Germany. Different and in a way more evil. For we used those lynchings as a kind of symbolic rite to keep alive in men's minds the idea of white supremacy and we set up a system of avoidance rites that destroyed not bodies but the spirit of men."

"I wonder how the Negroes felt," the girl whispered. "I've never thought about it before. But the children, how did it make them feel? I guess it is strange that I've never tried to imagine how they felt."

"I suppose there is no way you can feel it, truly, unless you live through it. We whites have a color glaze on our imaginations that makes it hard to feel with the people we have segregated ourselves from. But I think, as they watched the signs go up, and saw wall after wall built by law to shut them out from the life of their nation, that many of them blocked it off just as did white people. I think maybe they drew a little circle around their small personal lives and tried not to look beyond, for there were too many sinister sounds and shadows outside. They filled these small lives with work and raising their families and their hope of heaven and a struggle for education, and dancing and razor fights and dreams and laughter. And there was singing, the saddest singing in all the world, and the most beautiful. And sometimes we who caused the sadness would weep with them as they sang."

"The North can't understand that," she interrupted softly, "but I do. And I think it makes us seem a little more decent."

"Maybe it makes us only more complex. But anyway, most adjusted as quietly as possible and tried to make the best of the little they had. Sometimes they have been called Uncle Toms for this and 'handkerchief heads' and, nowadays, 'quislings' by some people in the North though I think they were only trying to hold on to sanity in a world of madness. And some, having been given an education, began to try to find a rational way out for their people. But a few angry bitter ignorant Negroes did fight back and in the only way they knew how: by assaulting white women. It didn't happen often but it happened and it was a powerful and suicidal revenge. White men had ruthlessly used Negro women for a hundred and fifty years and carelessly abandoned their children. It was natural that a few Negro men should try to hurt the white race in the same way they had been hurt. But it was like pouring gasoline on a fire. And every mind in the South was scorched by the heat.

"People said, 'You see? We have to have a lynching now and then. You see? This is why segregation is right!'

"Your parents and I lived our babyhood in those days of wrath. But always the violence was distant, the words vague and terrible for we were protected children. A lynching could happen in our county and we wouldn't know it. Yet we did know because of faces, whispers, a tightening of the whole town."

I did not say any more for a little for I was caught in those old days, remembering: Sometimes it was your nurse who made you know. You loved her, and suddenly she was frightened, and you knew it. Her eyes saw things that your eyes did not see. As the two of you sat in the sand playing your baby games, she'd whisper, "Lawd Jesus, when you going to help us!" And suddenly the play would leave the game and you would creep close to her begging her to shield you from her trouble. . . . Sometimes it would be your father, explaining a race incident to the older children. Even now I can feel that hush, the changed voices when they saw you listening, the talking down to the little one in false and cheerful words, saying, "Sugar, what you been playing today?"

So we suffered the grown folks' trouble, but without understanding. Cruel things were learned so casually. You would be in the buggy with your father, out near the turpentine still where the convict gang worked, as was done in those days, on your father's turpentine farm. A foreman would come over and make his report. "What he needs is the sweat box," sometimes he'd say of a troublesome Negro. And you'd sit there listening while chills curled over your body and mind. "No," your father would reply quietly, "we can't do that. Straighten him out in some other way." And you were glad that your father wouldn't let him do these things, but you had heard the word *sweat box* before you could spell it, and you knew some of your father's friends did use the sweat box or stocks or whipping as punishment for the convicts leased out to them and these same friends gave you and your little sister candy and dimes and sometimes brought you presents from Savannah. Strange, how you remember a little bag of candy and a sweat box together. . . .

I sat there facing the girl, thinking, feeling again the old guilt I had felt as a child though I had not known then why I felt it. But you shut the bad away so quickly and remembered only the pleasant, the games, great shadows of clouds moving across sunny grass, sugar cane and boiled peanuts and figs . . . odd wispy things . . . like sticking banana shrubs up your nostrils for the sweet smell of it, or taking a handkerchief full of them to teacher. These are the things white children remembered. It is so easy to see the old scuppernong vine which you used to climb in the hot sun, sitting there on top of the trellis eating grapes until tummies were tight and round, watching hens below peck up the pulps from the sand and gulp them with a quick turn of the head . . . soft glazey pulp, peck, gulp. . . . It is easy to see this. So hard to see Something swinging from a limb—because you never saw it. You only heard the whispers, saw the horror of it in dark faces you loved. Once I heard the thin cracking shots of a drunken farmer on Saturday, killing a Negro who had sassed him. Sometimes, when I am tired, those shots ring through my ears as if it had happened a few moments ago. But not often. There is too much that made me love the place where I was born, that makes me even now want to remember only the good things. . . .

The door closes so quickly. But when trouble blows hard, the door flies open, old fears creep out, giant fears, bigger now and greedier, having fed for many years on other anxieties that we shut up with them, when we were babies. People my age have memories like this, that can trample the reason down when there is talk of change or race violence.

"It isn't all greed," I heard myself say aloud, "though some still believe segregation pays."

She looked up quickly as if she too had forgot that we were talking.

"By the time we were as old as you," I continued, "things had quieted down. Race relations seemed 'settled.' Segregation had hardened around our lives and feelings like cement. The newspapers had worked out a system of leaving out everything that they thought would 'upset the people.' Many evil things happened down here but few knew about them. And this false peace gave an ease to men's minds. They could almost believe this life was good and right, and they hated anyone who disturbed this feeling.

"So we learned to do what southern tradition told us to do. Though our conscience sometimes hurt, we obeyed the laws. We did not use the word *dictator,* for we thought of ourselves as free Americans, but we obeyed this invisible power as meekly as if Hitler or Stalin had given the orders. It seemed to us that we had no other choice."

"But is it never to end?" she said. "It's like a nightmare that everybody is having together! I am glad to know how it started but who is going to stop it? Is it going on and on and on?"

"Not if your generation refuses to let it."

"But how can a person like me do anything! No matter how wrong you think it is, laws are against you, custom is against you, your own family is against you. How do you even begin? I guess," she said slowly, "if you hated your family, it would be easier to fight for what is right, down here. It would be easier if you didn't care how much you hurt them."

We had made the circle and were beginning that old treadmill route that the tortured southern liberal knows so well. We were tired, it was late. I told her we would talk again another time. I told her that there were ways out of the trap, that things were changing a little, that people could change anything, even segregation, and do it quickly if they really wanted to. . . . If they really wanted to. . . .

ᴧ 4 ᴧ

The Stolen Future

I HAVE never forgot that night and the girl's hurt questions, or those children and their little play or the way we fixed its ending to "make it happy," pretending a decency and grace that are against the laws of our region.

It seems such a little thing, doesn't it? A few children gathered on a mountain making a play about a child growing to maturity—a small play to be presented only before their parents—of Every Child living on a planet alone, who tries to reach out and embrace his universe and finds that he cannot because Religion will not show him the way, and Science is too busy with the making of machines and gadgets and bombs to use its resources to help him, and Conscience has learned no new lessons since childhood, and only Southern Tradition is strong and vigilant in acting out its beliefs.

Out of that play came questions asked by a young girl who used a young girl's words, but no wise man of our earth could have asked more important ones.

I had not tried to give her answers. I had tried only to

give her understanding of the difficulties of her elders—of all of us who have failed so miserably in the culturing of children. Knowing that bitterness is a poor bent key to use to unlock the old rusty door of human failure, I wanted her to begin her search for these answers with sympathy for those who had not found them. I knew the way would be hard enough for her who loved so passionately her ideals and a family that did not share them.

For twenty-five years a procession of children had come to our mountain, stayed a few summers, passed on. Sensitive, intelligent, eager for life, quick with their questions, generous and honest—fine raw material for the future. And so much of it had been wasted by a region that values color more than children.

I sat there thinking that night of those children—sleeping so quietly in little cabins under the trees. Though they had been shocked by this dilemma which their play had so suddenly exposed to their minds, most of them would soon forget. Busy with tennis and swimming and games they would forget that they had once wanted to play with all the world's children. And when they returned home it would be almost as easy as it had ever been to live the old segregated life. Though they would live it with as much kindness and grace as possible, they were too intimate a part of it, had been too rarely hurt by it, to fail to adjust harmoniously to it. They would content themselves with small acts of decency; they would oppose violence and vulgarity; they would want more things "for Negroes" and "for the poor" and would work for these things. But they would not reject the old way of life. Only a few would try to cut the umbilical cord.

Of those who believed they had done so, the more conspicuous would be the handful who would work with the

Communist party—believing this to be the only way to change things. Out of the hundreds of girls who have spent summers on the mountain, only a few have made this decision, but these few are important for us to consider for their number throughout our country is increasing.

These were young idealists who could not see that they had abandoned one iron box only to crawl into another for safety. One form of totalitarianism they had been born into and had accepted in childhood. They were too close to it to feel its basic similarities with another totalitarian system. All they could see was how ugly is the mask of white supremacy. This mask had the shadow of a dead man swinging across it; it was lighted up by cross burnings, streaked with the vulgarity and greed of decades of demagoguery and thievery, of dishonest state governments, of vast poverty, of men who sell their integrity for votes, twisted by a cruel disregard for the growth of the human spirit.

With memory full of such evils and their spirit revolting against them, the vague evils of the political system of Russia seemed far away. They could not realize in their imagination a country they had never visited, a vast, tumultuous revolution that had taken place before they were born and of which they had only hearsay reports. They had read of the millions in slave camps, of the firing line for leaders who deviated from the official party opinion, of the heavy suspicion under which every loyal Communist lives his life. Stories such as these were for them in the shadowland between fantasy and fact. Years of reading headlines and comic books, of seeing violence in movies, of listening to their own demagogues blow up big lies from small truths, had developed in them a resistance to believing anything which they had not come in actual contact with.

But they had come in contact with evils in their own region which were opposed not by democrats but by Communists and fellow travelers. Sometimes, they seemed the only ones who would speak clearly against them. The young people could not forget this. Wiser men than they, in authoritarian church as well as in political parties, have given up their integrity and freedom in order to abolish an evil that threatened the people's welfare.

Collaboration with communism seemed to these young Americans no risk. They took their freedom as for granted as the air they breathed. They could not conceive of its being withdrawn from them by any power on earth. At the same time, they resented being made to do wrong in the South, being compelled by law to go through doors marked *White*, being compelled by law to sit in the front of buses even though shamed by such vulgar and silly expression of arrogance. They were not proud of their parents who kept silent about segregation, and who postponed taking action in crises. They were young enough to feel change sweeping across the earth and they wanted heroism to march forth gallantly to meet it. But there was little heroism among the nice people they knew. There was only caution. They had read of the underground in Europe, of young people who worked together in what seemed to be a warm, thrilling camaraderie for goals that seemed good and right and who, tortured for their beliefs, had proudly died for them. These young southerners ached to risk something big for humanity but they knew that among their own people such heroes would be called only fools.

It was not that they had more love for their fellowmen than had tortured young liberals. Perhaps they had only more resentment. Perhaps because they had resented the "unfairnesses" of their own childhood they could identify more easily with unfair treatment of strangers. Whatever the names of the little seeds that had fallen in childhood soil, they had now sprouted into a sympathy for all men in trouble and an impatience with hypocrisy and inaction. It was a tragic thing to watch these young southerners move with so much valor from one little stage to another on which authority would once more play out its old drama and to know that they did so because in the strongest democracy on earth they were not free to live their ideals.

I have in front of me, as I write, a sheaf of clippings: words said by white men of the South. And as I turn these pages reading what the South's leaders have said I cannot forget all the South's children who have listened:

. . . But we will resist to the bitter end, whatever the consequences, any measure or any movement which would have a tendency to bring about social equality and intermingling and amalgamation of the races in our states.

—Senator Richard Russell,
during FEPC filibuster, 1946

. . . I would say to the Negro: before demanding to be a white man socially and politically, learn to be a white man morally and intellectually—and to the white man: the black man is our brother, a younger brother, not adult, not disciplined, but tragic, pitiable, and lovable; act as his brother and be patient.

—William Alexander Percy,
Lanterns on the Levee, 1941

Only a fool would say the Southern pattern of separation of the races can, or should be overthrown.

—*Atlanta Constitution*,
Editorial, Sept. 26, 1948

The yellow people, the brown people and the blacks are mentally unfit for directors in our form of government. You can-

not change these natural and God-ordained mental processes.
. . . When, and if, our voters' list contains a large percentage of
voters of other than Caucasian stock, then our constitutional form
of government becomes impossible and unworkable. . . . No
educational test will discern this natural difference in voters.

—Tom Linder, Georgia Commissioner of Agriculture,
in a letter to the *Atlanta Journal,* 1948

The permanent betterment of race relations cannot be brought
about unless the ground is cleared by recognition on the part of
both races that the problem will not yield to a cure-all solution,
and that the explosive issue of segregation must not be called into
question.

—David L. Cohn,
Where I was Born and Raised, 1948

The way to control the nigger is to whip him when he does not
obey without it, and another is never to pay him more wages than
is actually necessary to buy food and clothing.

—W. K. Vardaman, quoted by
W. J. Cash, *Mind of the South*

Whenever the Constitution [of the United States] comes between me and the virtue of the white women of the South, I say
to hell with the Constitution!

—Cole Blease, quoted by
W. J. Cash, *Mind of the South*

The Negro, not having assimilated the white man's ethics,
giving only lip service to the white man's morality, must for his
own peace and security accept whole-heartedly the white man's
mores and taboos.

—William Alexander Percy,
Lanterns on the Levee, 1941

I cannot emphasize one point too strongly. The white South
is as united as 30,000,000 people can be in its insistence upon
segregation. Federal action cannot change them. It will be tragic
for the South, the Negro, and the nation itself if the government
should enact and attempt to enforce any laws or Supreme Court

decisions that would open the South's public schools and public gathering places to the Negro.

—Hodding Carter,
Atlanta Journal, Sept. 3, 1948

Political equality means social equality and social equality means intermarriage, and that means the mongrelizing of the American race. . . . I cannot and will not be a party to the recognition of the Fourteenth and Fifteenth Amendments.

—Ellison D. Smith,
U.S. Congress, 1932

It is hard to forgive such words. But it is harder to forgive ourselves. For though we would not stoop to say them, we have let them be said in the hearing of southern children.

Why can words such as these, which our politicians use whenever the issue of civil rights comes up, stir such deep anxiety in men's hearts? How can one idea like segregation become so hypnotic a thing that it binds a whole people together, good, bad, strong, weak, ignorant and learned, sensitive, obtuse, psychotic and sane, making them one as only a common worship or a deeply shared fear can do? Why has the word taken on the terrors of taboo and the sanctity of religion? What makes it so important to us that men will keep themselves poor to sustain it, out of jobs to defend it? Why is it so sacred that the church has let it eat the heart out of religion? Why will not Christian ministers in the South—with the exception of a valiant handful—preach against it? Why is it that newspaper editors will not write editorials opposing it? The answer surely is worth searching for.

When Greenville taxicab drivers, Walton County lynchers, Toombs County jurors, Christian ministers, doctors, politicians, patients in mental hospitals and their attendants, writers, university presidents, union members and mill owners, newspaper editors, garbage collectors and Rotarians, rich and poor, men and women, unite in common worship and common fear of one idea we know it has come to hold deep and secret meanings for each of them, as different as are the people themselves. We know it has woven itself around fantasies at levels difficult for the mind to touch, until it is a part of each man's internal defense system, embedded like steel in his psychic fortifications. And, like the little dirty rag or doll that an unhappy child sleeps with, it has acquired inflated values that extend far beyond the rational concerns of economics and government, or the obvious profits and losses accruing from the white-supremacy system, into childhood memories long repressed.

Why is this so?

Why, said the girl, *does Daddy want to keep Negroes segregated—what pleasure does he get out of it? Does it make him richer to keep them that way?* . . .

Do you think we should break laws? she said. . . .

If they've made up their mind that the signs stay up and segregation is going to be here forever then why do they fool themselves? Why pretend and go to church and say nice words? It doesn't make sense. . . .

Since we have to practice segregation why didn't you make us believe it is right? When I have children I am not going to give them a single ideal they can't practice. . . .

If you hated your family it would be easier to fight for what is right down here. . . .

You cannot forget words like this if you have ever heard a young voice say them.

Part Two

The White Man's Burden Is His Own Childhood

~ 1 ~

The Lessons

IT BEGAN so long ago, not only in the history books but in our own childhood. We southerners learned our first three lessons too well.

I do not think our mothers were often aware that they were teaching us lessons. It was as if they were revolving mirrors reflecting life outside the home, inside their memory, outside the home, and we were spectators entranced by the bright and terrible images we saw there. The mirror might be luminous or streaked, or so dimmed that reflections were no more than shadows, but we learned from this preview of the world we were born into, what was expected of us as human creatures.

We were taught in this way to love God, to love our white skin, and to believe in the sanctity of both. We learned at the same time to fear God and to think of Him as having complete power over our lives. As we were beginning to feel this power and to see it reflected in our parents, we were learning also to fear a power that was in our body and to fear dark people who were everywhere around us, though the ones who came into our homes we were taught to love.

By the time we were five years old we had learned, without hearing the words, that masturbation is wrong and segregation is right, and each had become a dread taboo that must never be broken, for we believed God, whom we feared and tried desperately to love, had made the rules concerning not only Him and our parents, but our bodies and Negroes. Therefore when we as small children crept over the race line and ate and played with Negroes or broke other segregation customs that were known to us, we felt the same dread fear of consequences, the same overwhelming guilt that was ours when we crept over the sex line and played with our body, or thought thoughts about God or our parents that we knew we must not think. Each was a "sin," each "deserved punishment," each would receive it in this world or the next. Each was tied up with the other and all were tied close to God.

These were our first lessons. Wrapped together, they were taught us by our mother's voice, memorized with her love, patted into our lives as she rocked us to sleep or fed us. As the years passed, we learned other lessons and discovered interesting ways of cheating on them but these first rules of our life were sacred. They were taboos which we dared not break. Yet we did break them, for it was impossible to observe them. We broke the rules and told ourselves that we had kept them. We were not liars; we were human, and only used the ways that the human mind has of meeting an insoluble problem. We believed certain acts were so wrong that they must never be committed and then we committed them and denied to ourselves that we had done so. It worked very well. Our minds had split: hardly more than a crack at first, but we began in those early years a two-leveled existence which we have since managed quite smoothly.

The acts which we later learned were "bad" never seemed

really "bad" to us; at least we could find excuses for them. But those we learned were "bad" before we were five years old were CRIMES that we could not excuse; we could only forget. Though many a southerner has lived a tough hardened life since the days his mother rocked him until his eyes were glazed with sleep, his anxiety is, even now, cencerned largely with the moral junk pile which he wandered around in when a little child. But more important perhaps than the ethical residue left in our minds was the process of this learning which gave our emotions their Gothic curves.

Our first lesson about God made the deepest impression on us. We were told that He loved us, and then we were told that He would burn us in everlasting flames of hell if we displeased Him. We were told that we should love Him for He gives us everything good that we have, and then we were told that we should fear Him because He has the power to do evil to us whenever He cares to. We learned from this part of the lesson another: that "people," like God and parents, can love you and hate you at the same time; and though they may love you, yet if you displease them they may do you great injury; hence being loved by them does not give you protection from being harmed by them. We learned that They (parents) have a "right" to act in this way because God does, and that They in a sense represent God, in the family.

Sometimes, when we felt sore and weakened by anxieties that we had no words for, and battered by impulses impossible to act out, we tried to believe that God was responsible for this miserable state of affairs and one should not be too angry with parents. At least we thought this as we grew older and it helped some of us make a far more harmonious adjustment to our parents than to God.

As the years passed, God became the mighty protagonist of ambivalence although we had not heard the word. He loomed before us as the awesome example of one who injures, even destroys, in the name of "good" those whom He loves, and does it because He has the "right" to. We tried loyally to think of Him as our best friend because we were told that He was. Weak with fear, we told ourselves that when you break the rules you "should be punished" by Him or your parents. But a doubt, an earthy animal shrewdness, whispered that anyone who would harm us was also our enemy. Yet these whispers we dared not say aloud, or clearly to ourselves, for we feared that we might drop dead if we did. Even a wispy thought or two loaded us down with unbearable guilt. As we grew older and began to value reason and knowledge and compassion, we were told that He was wise and all-loving; yet He seemed from Old Testament stories to be full of whimsies and terrifying impulses and definitely not One whom a child could talk to and expect to receive an understanding reply from.

He was Authority. And we bowed before His power with that pinched quietness of children, stoically resigning ourselves to this Force as it was interpreted by the grown folks.

But life seemed a lost battle to many of us only after we learned the lesson on the Unpardonable Sin. Then it was that man's fate, our fate certainly, was sealed. According to this lesson, received mainly at revival meetings but graven on our hearts by our parents' refusal to deny it, God forgave, if we prayed hard and piteously enough, all sins but one. This one sin "against the Holy Ghost" He would never forgive. Committing it, one lived forever among the damned. What this sin was, what the "Holy Ghost" was, no one seemed to know. Or perhaps even grown folks dared not say it aloud. But the implication was—and this was made plain

—that if you did not tread softly you would commit this sin; the best way to avoid it was never to question anything but always accept what you were told.

Love and punishment . . . redemption and the unpardonable sin. . . . He who would not harm a sparrow would burn little children in everlasting flames. . . . It all added up to a terrible poetry and we learned each line of it by heart.

Our second lesson had to do with our body. It was a complicated one and bewildering, and was taught us as was our theology, in little slivers and by the unfinished sentence method. But we learned it as we learned all of our lessons, knowing they were important because of the anxious tones in which they were taught. This lesson, translated into words, went something like this:

"God has given you a body which you must keep clean and healthy by taking baths, eating food, exercising, and having daily elimination. It is good also to take pride in developing skills such as baseball and swimming and fighting, and natural to think a little about the clothes you wear. But your body itself is a Thing of Shame and you must never show its nakedness to anyone except to the doctor when you are sick. Indeed, you should not look at it much yourself, especially in mirrors. It is true that in a sense your body is 'yours' but it isn't yours to feel at home with. It is God's holy temple and must never be desecrated by pleasures—except the few properly introduced to you—though pain, however repulsive, you must accept as having a right to enter this temple as one accepts visits from disagreeable relatives.

"Now, parts of your body are segregated areas which you must stay away from and keep others away from. These areas you touch only when necessary. In other words, you cannot associate freely with them any more than you can associate freely with colored children.

"Especially must you be careful about what enters your body. Many things are prohibited. Among these, probably the easiest to talk about is alcohol. 'Drinking' is a symbol of an evil that begins so early in life that it may be 'inherited,' for one who 'drinks' moves almost from milk bottle to whisky bottle, from the shaky legs of a child to the shaky legs of a drunk. The word *prohibition* means a movement to prohibit strong drink but every one knows that stronger temptations are prohibited with it, just as one knows that *segregation* also shuts one away from irresistible evils. Indeed, prohibition and segregation have much to do with each other, for there are the same mysterious reasons for both of these restrictions. Food, however, is not restricted; you may eat it with a clear conscience and whenever you are hungry.

"As you are beginning to see, what enters and leaves the doors of your body is the essence of morality. Yet if you are a little girl, you should not be aware that there are certain doors. So this question of where babies come from turns into a complicated matter since it concerns both a private entrance and a semi-public exit which each human being has to make but no one wants to remember. It is true that girls are quite involved in this since most of them will some day be mothers but it is better just now for you (whether boy or girl) to accept the idea that storks bring babies, or if you prefer, that they are found in the doctor's bag. At least accept it until you are grown and can face up to the ugliness of the whole business of creation. (I have at moments wondered if moralists had only morals at heart or if they had also the self-esteem of little males in mind when they hid from children the facts of life, fearing perhaps that little females might over-value their role in this drama of creation and, turning 'uppity' as we say in Dixie, forget their inferior place in the scheme of things.)

"The truth of the matter is, that the world is full of secrets and the greatest of these are concerned with you and the feelings that roam around in you. The better part of valor is to accept these secrets and never try to find out what they are. Simply remember that morality is based on this mysterious matter of entrances and exits, and Sin hovers over all doors. Also, the Authorities are watching.

"Now, on the other hand, though your body is a thing of shame and mystery, and curiosity about it is not good, your skin is your consolation, your glory, and the source of your strength and pride. It is white. And, as you have heard, whiteness is a symbol of purity and excellence. Remember this: Your white skin proves that you are better than all other people on this earth. Yes, it does that. And does it simply because it is white—which, in a way, is a kind of miracle. But the Bible is full of miracles and it should not be too difficult for us to accept one more." (Southern children did not learn until years later that no one had thought much about skin color until three or four centuries ago when white folks set out from Europe to explore the earth. Nor did they know until they were grown that men in Europe and America had written books about it and a racial philosophy had developed from it which "proved" this Ptolemaic regress in which the white man was the center of the universe and all other races revolved around him in concentric circles. The racists "proved" the white man's superiority, especially the white Christian's, just as Ptolemy long before them had proved that the earth was the center of the universe, and as the theologians of the Middle Ages proved

that angels danced on the point of needles, and as Communists prove their fascinating theories that the world and all
within it revolve around Marxist economics.)

"Since this is so," our lesson continued, "your skin color is
a Badge of Innocence which you can wear as vaingloriously
as you please because God gave it to you and hence it is
good and right. It gives you priorities over colored people
everywhere in the world, and especially those in the South,
in matters of where you sit and stand, what part of town you
live in, where you eat, the theaters you go to, the swimming
pools you use, jobs, the people you love, and so on. But
these matters you will learn more about as you grow older."

Exaggerated? Perhaps. Whenever one puts a belief, a
way of life, into quick words of course one exaggerates.
Distortion, condensation, displacement are used not only
by artists and all of us in our dreams, they are used every
time we speak aloud. Yet when we thought about it at all
we southerners came close, in our thinking, to what I have
put down here.

This process of learning was as different for each child as
were his parents' vocabulary and emotional needs. We cannot wisely forget this. And we learned far more from acts
than words, more from a raised eyebrow, a joke, a shocked
voice, a withdrawing movement of the body, a long silence,
than from long sentences. But however skillfully our
grown-up minds have found euphemisms to cover brutali-
ties and gaucheries, however widely we now separate in
our memory one lesson from another to avoid their chilling
implications, we accepted with scarcely a differing shade
of emphasis the lesson outlines sketched here.

The lesson on segregation was only a logical extension of
the lessons on sex and white superiority and God. Not only

Negroes but everything dark, dangerous, evil must be pushed to the rim of one's life. Signs put over doors in the world outside and over our minds seemed natural enough to children like us, for signs had already been put over forbidden areas of our body. The banning of people and books and ideas did not appear more shocking than the banning of our wishes which we learned so early to send to the Darktown of our unconscious. But we clung to the belief, as an unhappy child treasures a beloved toy, that our white skin made us "better" than all other people. And this belief comforted us, for we felt worthless and weak when confronted by Authorities who had cheapened nearly all that we held dear, except our skin color. There, in the Land of Epidermis, every one of us was a little king.

Each lesson thus was linked on to the other, drawing strength from it. Indeed, the relentless interlocking of these learnings grows more and more clear as one retraces the paths and bypaths circling through a southern childhood. Forbidden sex play . . . forbidden dreams . . . forbidden relations . . . restlessness . . . resentment . . . guilt . . . emptiness. . . . *Ah there they are! The colored kids. Come on, you all, let's push 'em off the sidewalk. Chocolate drop chocolate drop chocolate drop.* . . . And the answering cry, *Yan yan yan crackers crackers yan yan yan.* . . . Struggle. Sudden strange struggle. Hot feelings pouring over you, driving you to push hard against wiry dark quickbreathing little bodies, push hard until they are off the sidewalk, off into sandspurs and dirt, sobbing angrily, *We'll get even with you you just wait we'll get.* . . . And your crowd, flushed and dazed, walk on, victors for a wan moment over something, you never know what. For you like the colored kids. You don't really mind their walking on the sidewalk. What is a sidewalk! Yet you had to do something and this thing, you knew, THEY WHO MAKE THE RULES would let you do. Though your own mother might scold you for fighting and pushing, if she knew, though your parents might say, "You cannot hurt their feelings, remember that! You must never push any one, no matter who it is," though your own parents might not approve, yet OTHER PARENTS seem to think pushing little Negroes into sandspurs funny, like tying tin cans to a dog's tail, and THEY WHO MAKE THE RULES seem not to mind at all.

Anyway, this pushing off the sidewalk is not one of the Sins you have to worry about. You somehow know this. Even if Mother doesn't approve, you know it isn't one of the Sins. You do not have to pray about it, for it has never been mentioned in church or Sunday school. You know you will not go to hell if you push little colored kids into sandspurs (or later out of jobs) though you may go there if you steal a nickel or do "bad" things or even think them. Now, if you were to go to church or to school with colored children, that would be worse than a sin, worse than anything you know of. You've learned that somewhere. But how could you do it anyway, for churches and schools would not let the colored kids in even if you would. . . . And then you grow confused and stop thinking and try never again, as long as you live, to think about it. But you have learned now to know a real sin from a mistake because of the look on faces when THEY talk to you about these matters. It is a secret, shamed look that creeps into their eyes as if THEY too have done naughty things and faces grow tight and worried. Sometimes all grown-up faces look worried as if something is going to happen that even THEY cannot keep from happening. As you lie awake at night thinking about it, you wonder why you never heard anyone talk calmly and pleasantly about the body or race, why no one has ever explained these interesting matters to you. Both are mysteries. Both have to do with Sin. And punishment for sin is inexorable.

This terrifying sense of disaster that will befall you if you do not learn your lessons hung over most of us. Here and there a few escaped it in homes of rare sophistication or rare rebellion. And often the favored child of a family was wrapped so securely in a sense of being cherished that the Danger seemed for him remote. But favored children of a home and homes favored by exceptional knowledge and good will could not escape the weight of taboo. It was, for them, padded with love and esteem and a regard for the amenities of the human spirit, and fell more gently on minds and hearts. But once under it, these children too were squeezed by its weight, shaped by it as were all until they, like the rest, became little crooked wedges that fit into the intricately twisting serrated design of life which THEY WHO MAKE THE RULES had prepared for us in Dixie.

Our mothers and fathers would have weakened, I think, had not religion and southern tradition kept them hard at the teaching. Even so, their hearts and their sense of humor gave us many a holiday. There were times when we were not southerner or sinner but just children playing and, like children everywhere, concerned only with making the whole world into a fine toy for our games.

Our parents did more. Their love and pity overwhelmed them, sometimes, after too many strict lessons (which they did not quite believe in), and they guiltily made it up to us, or to themselves, by indulging us in a startling fashion. Poor and rich parents did this. We were petted children, not puritans. Sugar-tit words and sugar-tit experiences too often made of our minds and manners a fatty tissue that hid the sharp rickety bones of our souls. *Honey, sugar, sweetie* were milk names that still cling to our middle-aged vocabulary. Kisses and big hugs, and soothing laps to nuzzle up in, and tea cakes and bread 'n' butter 'n' sugar, and cane syrup poured on hot buttered biscuit, and homemade ice cream and praise, gave a velvety texture to childhood which did not keep out the sharp stabs from the lessons but soften them now in our memory until we deny that we felt them at all. The air was so warm and melting . . . and piles of moss made such thick feathery play houses to romp on under oak trees . . . the stars were close in the night sky and everywhere the sweet smell of flowers . . . how can one dig down deep enough into such a childhood to find the sharp needling lessons that sometimes gave a death-prick to our souls!

Footnotes spring up like weeds in my mind as I write this. For always I remember the next-door neighbor who was different, the friend down the street, or a relative, who was as frugal with pet names and desserts and caresses as with money. The South has its share of tight-lipped, tight-hearted people who rigorously followed a tight little road map on the journey via Dixie to heaven and did not let either their love or their guilt buy indulgences for their children. Like Calvin, from whom so many of our southern precepts came, they bent every little wire in childhood and pinched it to a predestined shape. Nothing was too small to be the concern of these moralists. And yet sometimes their insistence on a frugal diet and frugal clothes and frugal pleasures and frugal use of money and frugal fantasies served as a pruning knife which, as in New England, brought forth a heavy crop of scholarship or missionary zeal.

And there were the families, like my own, whose lives were firmly triangulated on sin, sex, and segregation but who nonetheless were shown a way to become free again.

A poor way, perhaps—a giving of artificial legs to a child whose legs have been cut off—yet it helped us walk.

Our mother and nurse and grandmothers petted us. We were sugar-tit children who were given a deep and terrifying anxiety about sin as we were being coddled and comforted. And outside our home we moved in the rigid patterns of segregation that all white southerners live. But our father never stopped saying, and because he believed it, we also believed: that nothing is really important about a man except his being human; that no one should sink so low as to have an enemy; and that work is not only something we owe in payment to an earth that has given us so much, it is also fun.

Such flashes of sanity are not to be treated lightly either in a home or in a region. I know these beliefs are touched with paternalism and middle-class *oblige*. And I am aware also that they who think systems can be better than the people in the system would sneer at grace and good will. That an individual might try in his own personal life to pay back his obligation to past generations who have bestowed so much upon him seems only a romantic gesture to those who think change is brought about by new systems, not by the quality of human growth. Nonetheless, these three beliefs—in work owed to one's earth, in the destructiveness of hate, and in the value of the individual—were like yeast in soggy dough in my family. And there were families throughout the South, more than we have guessed perhaps, who were taught such extracurricular activities of the human spirit.

But when we stepped outside our homes, Custom and Church took charge of our education.

Every little southern town is a fine stage-set for Southern

Tradition to use as it teaches its children the twisting turning dance of segregation. Few words are needed for there are signs everywhere. *White . . . colored . . . white . . . colored . . .* over doors of railroad and bus stations, over doors of public toilets, over doors of theaters, over drinking fountains. Sometimes when a town could afford but one drinking fountain, the word *White* was painted on one side of it and *Colored* on the other. I have seen that. It means that there are a few men in that town whose memories are aching, who want to play fair, and under "the system" can think of no better way to do it. But in most towns with one fountain, only the word *White* is painted on it. The town's white idiot can drink out of it but the town's black college professor must go thirsty on a hot August day.

There are the signs without words: big white church on Main Street, little unpainted colored church on the rim of town; big white school, little ramshackly colored school; big white house, little unpainted cabins; white graveyard with marble shafts, colored graveyard with mounds of dirt. And there are the invisible lines that turn and bend and cut the town into segments. Invisible, but electrically charged with taboo. Places you go. Places you don't go. White town, colored town; white streets, colored streets; front door, back door. Places you sit. Places you cannot sit.

From the time little southern children take their first step they learn their ritual, for Southern Tradition leads them through its intricate movements. And some, if their faces are dark, learn to bend, hat in hand; and others, if their faces are white, learn to hold their heads high. Some step off the sidewalk while others pass by in arrogance. Bending, shoving, genuflecting, ignoring, stepping off, demanding, giving in, avoiding. . . . Children, moving through the labyrinth made by grown-up's greed and guilt and fear.

So we learned the dance that cripples the human spirit, step by step by step, we who were white and we who were colored, day by day, hour by hour, year by year until the movements were reflexes and made for the rest of our life without thinking. Alas, for many white children, they were movements made for the rest of their lives without feeling. What white southerner of my generation ever stops to think consciously where to go or asks himself if it is right for him to go there! His muscles know where he can go and take him to the front of the streetcar, to the front of the bus, to the big school, to the hospital, to the library, to hotel and restaurant and picture show, into the best that his town has to offer its citizens. These ceremonials in honor of white supremacy, performed from babyhood, slip from the conscious mind down deep into muscles and glands and on into that region where mature ideals rarely find entrance, and become as difficult to tear out as are a child's beliefs about God and his secret dreams about himself.

Southern Tradition taught well: we learned our way of life by doing. You never considered arguing with teacher, because you could not see her. You only felt the iron grip of her hand and knew you must go where all the other children were going. And you learned never, never, to get out of step, for this was a precision dance which you must do with deadly accuracy.

And as you went there were a few words, not many, that you never heard perhaps in your home but they became a chanting that accompanied this strange dance and vibrated with its movements: *Nigger, darkie, never call one mister, never call one mister, but would you want your sister, your sister, 300 years from savagery, states' rights states' rights, invading the home, danger our women our women.* Words that made no sense but beat like jungle drums on nerve endings. White words, that the drum-beaters never let die into silence. There were black words, too: *Yassir boss, yassir boss, howdy mistis, howdy,* words spoken loud and bendingly. *Now ain' dat right, yes mam!* followed by sleazy laughter that turned human dignity into a limp thing. But you liked it. And you felt big, important, superior even, as you heard it, though you might not be able to read or write. There were other words you did not hear and yet somehow you knew they were said: *Lord God that white man. Now don' he think he's somepin! Crackers. Stinking white crackers! Mind your manners but don't trust a one of 'em, hear! Mind your manners, child, or you won't live to be grown. Jesus, how I hate white folks, how I hate them!* Words that would have caused a colored man to die had he said them in the wrong place and yet you knew he said them.

These things you knew as you knew your own name. But Southern Tradition did not think it enough. One day, sometime during your childhood or adolescence, a Negro was lynched in your county or the one next to yours. A human being was burned or hanged from a tree and you knew it had happened. But no one publicly condemned it and always the murderers went free. And afterward, maybe weeks or months or years afterward, you sat casually in the drugstore with one of those murderers and drank the Coke he casually paid for. A "nice white girl" could do that but she would have been run out of town or perhaps killed had she drunk a Coke with the young Negro doctor who was devoting his life in service to his people.

So Southern Tradition taught her bleak routines with flashes of lightning to quicken our steps.

◡ 2 ◠

Trembling Earth

WE CANNOT understand the church's role as a teacher of southern children without realizing the strength of religion in the lives of us all, rich and poor. Whether we lived in a big house on College Street, a cottage on the side street or a shanty in mill town, most of us loved church. Sunday was a fiesta, a time for our prettiest dresses, the only day of the week when we wore hats, the only time in summer when little boys slicked back their hair and put on their shoes. And the only day when the church bells rang, Baptist and Methodist, clashing their sounds together in friendly proselyting.

I do not remember that we felt a profound reverence for the Unknown when we entered our church, or that our hearts stretched to touch something bigger than the mind can find words for. I am afraid we were too busy looking at each other's clothes or watching the veins swell out on old Mr. Amster's neck as he sang the Gloria, or staring at little Mr. Pusey as he led the tenors through the vagaries of the anthem.

Church was our town—come together not to kneel in worship but to see each other. God was our Host, we were guests in His House, the altar flowers were fresh and fragrant, and if it was Communion Day the cloth was starched and white and the silver cup out of which every one drank was shining. And though we willingly listened to the sermon if it was not too long, and felt a deep flowing sense of togetherness when we sang the Doxology, we were there also to mend the little broken places in our knowledge of each other.

To children, church was more interesting than school, for the grown folks were there and one's eyes could not get enough of their movements, their quick glances, the sudden stiff droop of those who fell asleep under the minister's soothing words. We liked to be with them. But we liked best of all, classes at Sunday school where we said the golden text and emptied our mite boxes and repeated the stories of Daniel in the lion's den and David and his slingshot.

After church, there would be a good dinner at home, and always guests could be invited.

It was a day set aside, made special, with no empty moment in it. Sunday school, morning worship, junior choir practice, and a walk in the woods to pick violets.

In a few homes, like my own, it was also a time when your father heard you name the books of the Bible, or listened encouragingly as you repeated ten Psalms from memory, or asked you odd questions about the old Prophets and tripped you flat with verses whose source you must identify. But we liked the old mouth-filling names, the strange adventures which the Israelites had, and the indignant invectives so eloquently hurled by the prophets at the weak ones on that long troubled journey that seemed never to end but went on from Sunday to Sunday.

The revival meetings in August were different.

The church's emphasis on revival meetings and the revival's effect upon southern personality are difficult to understand unless we let our minds fill with echoes of distance and darkness and ignorance and violence and worn-out bodies and land. For all are tied up with each other and have much to do with the quality of the southern conscience that is stretched so tightly on its frame of sin and punishment and God's anger.

Belief in Some One's right to punish you is the fate of all children in Judaic-Christian culture. But nowhere else, perhaps, have the rich seedbeds of Western homes found such a growing climate for guilt as is produced in the South by the combination of a warm moist evangelism and racial segregation. This flowering of revivals, conversions, deathbed repentance, mourners' bench, love feasts, and fundamentalism must be credited in part also to the historical circumstance of the Brothers John and Charles Wesley's and George Whitfield's visits to Georgia. We can hardly overestimate the influence of these three preachers of God on the mind of the South, for they were men of powerful personality, burning with a powerful belief in the importance of the common man's uncommon soul, and a powerful talent for making men believe in their soul's sacredness by giving size to their sins. It was a curious inversion, this proving a man's stature by the great black shadow he cast, but it worked. Men believed in their importance by believing in the importance of their sins and grew a pride in possessing a conscience that persecuted them.

These young giants of Methodism—not long out of Oxford and full of their discovery of the poor man's soul—came to the New World with their new way of preaching that was intimate and direct and deeply sincere. They went straight to the anxiety in the minds of these tough settlers and whipped it up to a froth that obliterated rational processes, then released them from it by showing them a clear narrow road to salvation. Circuit riders who followed them for more than a century continued this emphasis on the rebirth of the soul, as they moved from settlement to settlement preaching the Gospel. They were brave, tireless, passionate men who traveled on horseback, like old Peter Cartwright, three hundred miles a week, preaching four or five times a week, sometimes two or three times a day. Devoted to God and terrified of Him, they made Him into the Despot the people had left behind them when they fled Europe; and by threats of hell, they turned the rebels once more into meek lambs. They did far more than this of course, for men *were* reborn; they did, as it were, re-enter their mother's womb, and many of them found a peace that was real and a way of life that added kindness and decency to a South that had much too little of either.

The loneliness, ignorance, and isolation of the rural South made these old preachers welcome everywhere. In spite of their lashing sermons—perhaps because of them—wherever they went, the crossroads saloonkeeper vied with pillars of the church for the privilege of putting them up for the night, for all were hungry for news of a world they were completely cut off from, and fascinated by the power of men who believed and lived their belief.

They were brave men, these circuit riders, who could kill a rattler or swamp panther or wild turkey with casual accuracy or throw a drunken bully out of their meeting with no more than a comma's pause in their sermon. They were veterans pioneering for God, taking danger and death as quietly as they took their sleep. When they spoke, men listened. They preached on the sins that tough frontiersmen committed: drinking, fighting to kill, fornication, self-abuse, gambling, and stealing. And because they made these sins of heroic size by a passionate eloquence that modern preachers cannot equal, no other sins have ever seemed real to the southern imagination but become merely vexatious problems that do not belong in church. They preached, at times, of Jesus too and his love, and turned their brush-arbor congregation into wistful blubbering children who, there in the lonely woods, wept for something lost that they knew they could never find again on this earth but hoped to find in heaven.

Such men there were in both Methodist and Baptist churches (whose combined membership is about eighty per cent of the South's churchgoing people)—eloquent, fiery, compelling—and for more than a century they shaped and gave content to the conscience of southerners, rich and poor.

Camp meetings and revivals are the South's past, and once were a heroic part of that past. Today, though often cheapened and vulgarized to the point of obscenity, they are still part of the South's present. Guilt was then and is today the biggest crop raised in Dixie, harvested each summer just before cotton is picked. No wonder that God and Negroes and Jesus and sin and salvation are baled up together in southern children's minds and in many an old textile magnate's also.

When I was a child the annual revivals were a source of enormous terror and at the same time a blessed respite from rural monotony. Nothing but a lynching or a political race-hate campaign could tear a town's composure into as many dirty little rags or give as many curious satisfactions. Like political demagogues, the evangelists enjoyed people. And, like them, they won allegiance by bruising and then healing a deep fear within men's minds. They loved God too, but they feared Him far more than they loved Him and they urgently wanted their fellowmen to be saved from His wrath.

They believed their way of salvation was "right," as did the
old circuit riders, and could not conceive of another way of
avoiding destruction. And their faith released an enormous
energy which in most of us is locked tight in a struggle between the two halves of our nature.

They preached asceticism but preached it with the liber-
tine's words. And, as they preached, they looked as unlike an
ascetic as you can imagine. These were potent men—anyone
is wrong to think otherwise—who used their potency in their
ardent battle for souls.

How can such men be called hypocrites, as they are grossly
represented by most novels and plays written about them?
They have had numerous counterfeit followers who were—
mean nasty tight men who today wander up and down Tobacco Road in Dixie and Tobacco Road in Detroit spreading
their gospel of fear and hate; men who preach more against
the evils of communism than the evils of sex but are concerned almost wholly with these two "sins." These are the
rotted culls of an evangelism that once was a respected and
important part of protestant religion.

The revivalists I knew as a child lived their religion as they
saw it and lived it honestly. It is true that they were ambivalent men who had healed themselves by walling off one
segment of their life and who kept many doors open in their
personality by keeping one door securely locked. And they
were men whose powerful instincts of sex and hate were
woven together into a sadism that would have devastated
their lives and broken their minds had they acknowledged
it for what it was. Instead, they bound it into verbal energy
and with this power of the tongue they drove men in herds
toward heaven, lashing out at them cruelly when they
seemed to be stampeding, persuading them with laughter
and tears when they moved in the right direction but too

slowly. And in doing this, they felt that they were doing God's will. They were saving souls and they believed that any method was justified, if by using it, they could say, "Here, Lord, is one more for Thy Kingdom."

They were sincere if ham actors—a few of them almost touched greatness now and then—and they brought to a South bereft of entertainment and pleasure a brief surcease from the gnawing monotony that ate our small-town lives away. They often presented this entertainment with style and always with drama, for they were unafraid to explore the deep forbidden places of man's heart. There are few artists today who would dare probe so ruthlessly the raw sores of our life as did these evangelists, though they ignored the patterns of culture and the profound needs that produced the sores. They were not wise men but they were shrewd in the use of mob psychology. They were curiously indifferent to cultural patterns or else in violent loyalty defended the barbed wires crisscrossing our age on which their own lives had been wounded. And they could turn into stupid foolish men when confronted with questions that ask "Why?" Wherever their answers came from, that place did not send them answers to the problems of poverty, of race segregation, unions, wages, illness and ignorance, war, and waste of forest and soil and human relations, or answers to the old question of human freedom which Jesus turned around and around until its light blinded men with fury and drove them to build institutions to shut out its shining.

Their religion was too narcistic to be concerned with anything but a man's body and a man's soul. Like the child in love with his own image and the invalid in love with his own disease, these men of God were in love with Sin that had come from such depths within that they believed they had created it themselves. This belief in the immaculate conception of Sin they defended with a furious energy and stubbornly refused to assent to the possibility that culture had had any role in its creation.

They were twisted men, and often fanatics, but they were delightful companions. I know this is true, for many of the southern revivalists whose names all Methodists know were guests in our home for the duration of the August revival. These men were remarkable storytellers, with a warm, near-riotous sense of humor; brilliantly adept with words, soft and gentle with the children of their host, and courteous and considerate of their hostess. We liked them. My mother and father, neither of whom was easily drawn to the mediocre, respected them. We admired them and were influenced by them, for they had two of the essential qualities of leadership: They were free of personal anxiety, and they were close to their instinctual feelings. They were saved men. And they were sure of it. At the same time, what they were "saved from" was still accessible to them. The return of the repressed, which most of us puny folk fear as we fear the ghosts of our beloved, were to these powerful evangelists something they could whistle back at will, giants made impotent by the "power of God." No wonder they hypnotized us all!

They were fine looking men, strong, bold, with bodies of athletes. They had to be, for they put themselves through a killing routine: three sermons a day, with prayer circles before breakfast and midday dinners with the town's leading citizens at which every one gorged himself on fried chicken, corn and okra and butter beans, iced tea, peach ice cream, and lemon cheese cake; and after the evening sermon, an altar service which was often prolonged for hours by those under conviction of sin who agonized and prayed and yet could not secure release from their guilt. I shall never forget how I suffered with these strong men of our town—the butcher or the pitcher on the baseball team or the tenor in the choir—as they knelt there sobbing like children. Strangely enough, I cannot remember one time when the banker or millowner or principal of the school, or cotton broker or politician went to the altar. They were always among "the saved." Perhaps it is as well—for one little penitent journey might have caused a run on the bank or a cultural panic.

What an awesome gift these revivalists possessed for palpating the source of our anxiety! By means of threats, hypnotic suggestion, and a recall of the earliest fears of childhood, they plunged deep into our unconscious and brought up sins we had long ago forgotten. There were few of us whose souls did not pale out in the sulphurous glow of their sermons. Though they knew no word of psychoanalysis, they directed their attention to buried memories quite as much as the Freudians do, though the process was more like a butcher with a cleaver than a surgeon performing a skilled and delicate operation.

I have sometimes wondered why there were not suicides afterward, for surely enough terror and anxiety were released in unstable personalities to produce a collapse of the will to live. Perhaps we were saved from self-destruction simply because no matter how miserable and torn we were, life in Dixie seemed far better to the most unstable of us than any possible satisfactions that might accrue from succumbing to death wishes. For men believed in hell after death in those days and the belief restrained many a potential suicide from that infantile act of getting even with his world or himself. The revivals probably drove many more than we know into mental hospitals and into less conspicuous, because ambulatory, illnesses.

But when we were children, we did not analyze the motivations and consequences and costs of revivals, we accepted them. Hymns, sermons on hell, invitations (called "propositions") to come to the altar and be saved, the dirge-like singing that embroidered our nerves, the revivalist's soft whispers and prayers when one finally broke down and went scuttling to kneel at the altar—all of these phenomena we accepted with what seems, as I think of it now, a most extraordinary flexibility. There were such generous compensations: the sheet-lightning glimpses into the dark places of the human mind, the very real sense of being "saved," and scene after scene of drama and farce when an individual, strong in his refusal to give up his right to sin stood night after night adamant to the preacher's pleading though sometimes his name was called aloud.

This was strong meat for children but we loved it. There was excitement too in the setting of big tent, lanterns swinging high in the shadows, fresh clean smell of sawdust that covered the ground to make a suitable place for kneeling in prayer. There were always on the platform two pianos, and two pianos to small children were of the same exciting stuff as calliopes. There was a singer too who led the congregation with fine sweeping gestures that turned old hymns into hit tunes.

For a town whose opera house rarely had the spider webs dusted out, whose citizens depended for theater on the annual play given by the high school, and for gaiety on a minstrel show and a circus each winter, the big tent was a magnet which drew not only the rural folks but the most literate and wealthy from Main Street.

Once in the tent, we were shown monstrosities that Mr. Barnum would not have dared exhibit to his gawking audiences. Queer misshapen vices, strange abnormal sins were marched out before our young eyes, amazing, titillating us as no circus could do. We learned about the horrors of delirium tremens and the lush temptations that scarlet women dangle before men's eyes. *Whore, harlot, unnatural sins, self-abuse*—words which we had never heard in our homes and would not have dared repeat outside the church, became an August vocabulary that was pressed deep in our memory. Adolescents, whose parents could not bring themselves to tell them where babies came from, sat on the edge of benches, wet-lipped and tense, learning rococo lessons in Sin from the revivalist who seemed magnificently experienced in such matters. The sermon titled *For Men Only* lifted the lid from the flaming pit of things one should not know. And even little girls and their mamas safe at home watched eagerly for bits of ash that might fall from the big fire.

For the adventurous, such sins as these became irresistible. Any risk, even of hell, was worth running if one could but taste of this steamy dish which the preacher held so close, daring you, with awful threats of punishment, to touch. But for the tender-minded, the sensitive, the dish turned to vomit, and sometimes all of life seemed as nasty, as dangerous, as this portion of it with which so many sermons were concerned. Children without one protest quietly locked doors they had almost opened, forever shutting out life's natural spontaneous rhythms and curiosities.

In the sermons for children which revivalists customarily held in the afternoons, a lighter tone was sustained. The presence of little girls, sitting so stiffly in front of them with flushed-up cheeks and tight pigtails, may have made them a bit shy about pushing matters too ruthlessly. Or perhaps they needed to relax from their major efforts. Whatever their reasons, they made of the children's services rather pleasant divertisements, full of games and animal stories. We laughed on these afternoons, I remember that. Sin was shrunken to a stature that our small egos could cope with. The preacher quoted more from the New Testament than from the Old, and that was a relief. Many words about love were said, and few about vengeance. We were told that Jesus came to earth because God so loved the world that He gave His only begotten Son—which seemed to us a fine thing for God to do. We were told that Jesus loved us, that He was gentle, that soft little lambs curled up at His feet without fear, that He said, "Suffer little children to come unto Me." And for one radiant, luminous moment we knew Jesus, whatever The Rest did, would never hurt us for our mistakes. We gratefully sang, "What a Friend we have in Jesus," and cheerily piped, "Brighten the corner where you are," and gradually every one of us whose viscera had been squeezed into tight little knots by the threats of everlasting torture heard at the grown-up services, grew limp and sleepy and went home quietly and ate a good supper.

It was late at night, after the evening sermon with its persistent propositions and compulsive songs like "Almost persuaded . . . almost, but lost"; it was after the preacher had sent the town home vibrating with guilt and fear, after the grown folks were asleep and so remote from us who lay terribly awake; it was then that we remembered the threats. Then, in the darkness, hell reached out bright long red fingers and seared the edge of our beds. Sometimes we would doggedly whisper to ourselves, "We are saved too," but even as we said it, we believed ourselves liars. I remember how impossible it was for me to feel "saved." Though I went up to the altar and stayed until the revivalist pried me off my knees, I was never convinced that my kneeling had effected a change in either my present or future life. But sometimes, wanting it so badly, I lied and stood up with the rest when the evangelist asked all who were sure that they would go to heaven to arise and be counted. My younger sister, more certain of her place in the family, was naturally more certain of her place in heaven, and rarely went to the altar. I remember how I admired her restraint.

But even she shivered as the Unpardonable Sin, cold, silent, implacable, slid through the room just before we fell asleep. I can feel it even now, coiling around our memories like the rattlesnakes we had seen under palmettos, daring us to believe, as we lay there listening to the rustling of our past, that we had a chance at eternal life. Whatever the theologians thought about this most cruel of human ideas, which grew through the centuries into a dragon that devoured the minds of the children of Christendom, to me as a child the Unpardonable Sin had to do with one's forbidden dreams. And I think many other children shared this feeling that somehow it was tangled up with our secret hates and loves and all the passional temptations that tear at the human heart when it is three and four years old. The poets have sometimes viewed it as man's defiance of God as he stubbornly wrests from Him His knowledge of the universe, but we children thought of it more simply, and perhaps more profoundly, in terms of our own small past, and trembled, knowing our guilt.

So our learnings on sin and sex, often taught gently at home, were welded together by the flames of hell. Always we had the feeling of punishment about to fall upon us.

We too were "under arrest," we too were being tried. We never knew our crime, we never saw the Authorities face to face, but we knew we would ascend from court to court to higher court, like Kafka's Joseph K., and only death would yield up the final verdict.

No wonder we children feared Death as if he lived next door! For always he was slyly reaching out to snag our lives on his bony fingers if we once passed him carelessly. Graveyards full of baby dreams planted themselves in our past and stayed there, mouldering greenly. Tombstones stiffened in our minds, carving their inscriptions restlessly at night when we could not sleep. Born . . . died . . . born . . . died. We sometimes did not know how we were born, but we knew how we would die. And the littlest of us knew what might happen to us after death. Thinking of death sometimes made the living of life seem vague and shadowy as if it were no more than a few dark steps through the swamp that led toward eternal ——. We could never finish that sentence. It hung in our minds, curving into a big question-mark, and sometimes wrapping itself around our spirit until we could not move.

Our old nurse would say, "Law, honey, hit'll all change up deah. When us gets to heaven everything'll be right. Hit'll be right, honey," and she'd say it when she was moaning her own trouble with her husband or white folks and say it when she was picking sandspurs out of our bare feet. And sometimes we white children nestling close against the warm soft breasts of these strong old women could almost believe in the colored folks' heaven but more often with a passion for hopelessness we believed in the white folks' hell.

And everywhere there were the ghosts wandering restlessly through our everyday lives. Stories about haunted houses on the edge of town—what southerner does not remember!—merely took our minds off our own haunted lives and gave us reasons for our fears. We gratefully accepted the ghosts because they did give names to our fears and we urged the grown-ups to tell us again and again about them. And sometimes we learned to lay these ghosts by resurrecting them at will. We even grew fond of them as we walked the lonely curving paths across our trembling earth and felt them following us, like invisible pet dogs, wherever we went.

The physical setting for these tangled dreams and anxieties, the place we lived, was a backdrop to our Deep South childhood that seemed no more than a giant reflection of our own hearts. Back of our little town was the swamp, tangled green, oozing snakes and alligators and water lilies and sweet-blooming bays, weaving light and shadow into awful and tender designs, splotching our lives with brightness and terror. Green cypress blowing through the memory, held firmly to the past by its dark old knobby knees lost in brown water . . . rivers that go underground and creep up miles away . . . earth that shakes as you walk carefully on it, in swamp and edge of old moss-shadowed lakes.

This is the South I knew as a child. Swamp and palmetto and "sinks" and endless stretches of pines slashed and dripping their richness into little tin cups that glint like bright money. Twisting sand roads . . . warm soft sand that you play in; quicksand in which you die. Fields that flatten the eye until there is no curve left in it. Rows of crazy-leaning little grey shanties pushed over by the years. Cows wandering slow through palmetto, across the roads, mute and gaunt like the acres of stumps that do not move but stare at you like the cows. The hills were there, too, but beyond us. And beyond us were bright rolling lands that hold the sun in winter and red gullied earth so beautiful in its injury. All this is the South that we remember, curving gently and more and more steeply until stopped by mountains. Beyond the mountains was the North: the Land of Damyankees, where live People Who Cause All of Our Trouble; and at the end of the North was Wall Street, that fabulous crooked canyon of evil winding endlessly through the southern mind which is, like the dark race, secretly visited by those who talk loudest against it.

Our lessons were learned against this backdrop which rubbed on the senses day in, day out, confirming all that our feelings told us was true of life.

Here also, we unlearned our lessons.

~3~

Three Ghost Stories

THE RAVELING out of what had been woven so tightly together was usually a slow process. One thread at a time came loose. Then another. Sometimes a great hole was torn in it by a quick stabbing experience. However it happened, it was not long in the little southerner's life before the lessons taught him as a Christian, a white man, an American, a puritan, began to contradict each other.

Sometimes, it was as if he were surrounded by characters in a bad dream who pull him this way and that, crowd down on him until he is almost smothered, then suddenly move in opposite directions, dragging him with them. And always, standing by, were his parents telling him this bad dream is life and he must accept it; telling him, gently or sternly, that this is reality.

But gradually, in the way of all flesh, the southern child adjusted himself to his world in which people said what they did not mean, and meant what they dared not say.

As I try to measure and weigh the forces that pressed down on these children of my generation I am aware that

109

I am essaying an impossible task. We know that each personality creates its own gravitation system. A force that weighs heavily on one is without weight on another due to ten thousand differences in infantile experiences, in ego and conscience strength, in psychic energy and that indefinable something we call the capacity for survival.

Despite these differences, I think most of us found it more painful to adjust to the conflict set up in our personal relationships than to warring ideas or even to the restrictions put upon bodily drives, though here again one is dealing with imponderables and perhaps it is not fruitful to compare them.

The ideas, denying each other, we could bend to with relative ease, usually. Sometimes by acquiring an intellectual tone deafness we could keep ourselves from hearing, or hearing simultaneously, the antiphonal choruses of white supremacy and democracy, brotherhood and segregation, love and lynching, and so on. The human mind finds it an easy thing to split itself into what we used to call "logic-tight compartments." This separation divorced our beliefs from the energy that would have carried them into acts, but we accepted this moral impotence as a natural thing and often developed what is called a "judicious" temperament from believing equally in both sides of a question.

The instinctual drives of the body were more difficult to cope with. These were mighty feelings and no words could have stopped them. Only a fear of consequences more violent than desire could dam up these somatic urges. But our early training had given us plenty of fear—both of displeasing those we loved, and of eternal punishment. And it worked. This energy of course was only deflected—had it not found a way out, the personality would have exploded in madness. But there were outlets: substitute satisfactions, neuroses, a thousand ways in which the personality, like a mountain stream, twisted and turned, went underground, came up again in a remote place, rushed over rocks, wasted itself, but finally reached, somehow, the end of its journey.

This training given my generation, and its results in the shaping of personality, is different only in degree from that given most white Protestants throughout the Western world. (I separate Protestant from Catholic just here not because the training of Catholic children was less severe—on the contrary it was more so—but because the Catholic child was given in its religion more adequate compensations for its renunciations than were given little Protestants.) But though we learned and unlearned many lessons that will seem familiar to men and women of Christian background wherever they live in the Western world, and had in common with them the same twisting love-hate-guilt ties with our parents which psychoanalysis has made familiar to modern man as the Oedipus complex, we of the South also have had three traumatic relationships not common outside our region, that have left a lasting impression on all of our people, though few of us, actually, have suffered them directly.

These ghost relationships of long ago, that still haunt the southern mind, arouse so much terror and anxiety that many of today's most urgent problems cannot be dealt with rationally, even though the outcome of the world's present crisis may depend largely upon how they are solved. They are ghosts that must be laid, and I think perhaps the only way this can come about is for us to uncover them and see for ourselves the dusty nothingness beneath their terrifying masks.

These strange and twisted relationships interlock and no one of them can be understood without understanding all three. Perhaps the one that has touched most lives is the back-yard temptation that pulled for a century and a half at our Anglo-American grandfathers. By the historical "accident" of slavery, our slaveholding puritan ancestors were juxtaposed to a dark people, natural, vigorous, unashamed, full of laughter and song and dance, who, without awareness that sex is "sin," had reached genital maturity. These so-called primitives (whose culture had so many sophisticated elements in it) were not, we must remember, brought into this country and hidden away in ghettos. They were brought into our back yards and left there for generations. They were everywhere, and highly conspicuous not only because of their color but because of their liveliness which the chains of slavery never subdued. From all that we know of them they seem to have had, even as some have now, a marvelous love of life and play, a physical grace and rhythm and a psychosexual vigor that must have made the white race by contrast seem a washed-out people, drained of so much that is good and life-giving, and left with so little save their guilt and greed and aggression. It was natural that the white man was drawn to them. Laughter, song, rhythm, spontaneity were like a campfire in a dark tangled forest full of sins and boredom and fears. So bright, so near. . . .

But the back-yard temptation was also a menace—not so much a "menace to our women" (that poisonous idea flowered later) but a menace to the basic beliefs of white culture. In the front yard was a patriarchal system; in the back yard a matriarchy. In the front yard the lessons on sin, sex, and segregation and the value of money were taught, in the back yard the children seemed always to be having recess from lessons, and for reasons no one could understand were healthy and serene in nature, less aggressive, less greedy than the white children. In the big white house a white lady was corseting her feelings and those of her children in an effort to be "pure"—and settling back finally in flabby ignorance. But in the back yard, life went on, naked and unashamed. Little black children did all the naughty things little white children were punished for, did them and prospered in body and mind. I am not forgetting that they were slaves or that they worked long hours and were brutally driven on many plantations. I am here concerned not with how the white man treated the Negro, but with how the Negro treated himself and especially how black mothers treated their children. For there is a story here, that we know only in fragments, which is surely worth the telling.

I think these old black matriarchs knew secrets of child rearing and secrets of sanity that our psychiatrists have been learning the hard way for the past sixty years through research, and that white mothers still know too little about. Unconfused by a church's rigid system of splitting spirit from body and injecting sin into bodily needs, unconfused by a patriarchal-puritanic system which psychically castrated its women, who in turn psychically castrated their children, male and female, by the burden of anxiety they laid on their minds—these women knew intuitively, or from old lore, the psychosomatic truths that we whites are groping awkwardly toward today. The results in their children were a stability, a health, a capacity for accepting strain, an exuberance, and a lack of sadism and guilt that no Anglo-Saxon group, to my knowledge, has ever shown.

It is a pity that we do not know more about it. For these were mothers who, under a harsh regime, worked the miracle of rearing children who grew up to be neither psychic slaves nor psychic rebels. Throughout the ordeal of slavery they remained people of easy dignity, kindly, humorous, bending only when necessary, deeply hurt and sad (as their spirituals make us know), but sane at the core as neither a vengeful nor a cringing people can be. They developed severe faults, of course, during these centuries. Easy lying, deceit, flattery became almost second nature to many of them. But they flattered with their tongues in their cheeks, and their "lies" turned into an art form that has contributed richly to our literature. There were the exceptions: crazed individuals who ran amok; others who turned their hate upon themselves and members of their own race with their Saturday night razor fights and quick killings over trifles; still others there were who brazenly exploited their own shame, pawning their dignity for profit. But as a group they retained an amazing stability throughout days of slavery and even through much of the long readjustment following it. That it is fast disappearing today is one of the ironic results of an "education" given in our country that does not fit psychosomatic needs of Negroes any more than it has fitted the psychosomatic needs of white people and which is rapidly transforming many Negroes, restive under severe restraints and humiliations, into as aggressive and bitter a people as are many of the white group.

But throughout slavery they possessed a psychological quality that could maturely withstand the temptation to take revenge. Their record during the Civil War and later during the chaos of Reconstruction is one of the honorable in human annals. To call them cowards for not being vengeful, as some do today, is to ignore the dynamics of personality. Cowards would have been the first to let their hate feelings break through: it would not have required much bravery to kill and burn and rape helpless women and children left isolated on the big plantations. I think the answer lies in the home, in what happened between mother and child in those tiny slave cabins. Those of us who in our childhood knew a few of these strong old women—the children of slaves—can never forget their wisdom, their capacity for accepting life and people, their deep laughter, their unashamedness. They had strong instinctual feelings, not all of them loving, but they rarely let hate or fear master them. And I cannot imagine one of them feeling guilt in the way in which the white race feels it, nor do I remember their suffering from that sickness of the soul we now call ambivalence.

What the white race termed "savagery" in slaves who were so much less cruel than their masters, was due to a method of child-rearing which was probably common to many African cultures and which today we moderns are accepting as the "modern way of child guidance." But to our grandfathers this "method," with its cheerful results, was a threat to their own system of punishment and sin and guilt. And yet there these black women were in the back yard, turning white beliefs into silly lies, and tempting men beyond their endurance.

Temptation and menace began to twist together as they seesawed in the white man's mind. Attraction, fear, repulsion, attraction—so it went. After a few years, lighter faces began to appear here and there in back yards. More and more light faces. And, at the same time that they were finding the back-yard temptation irresistible, these white men were declaring and sometimes beginning to believe that Negroes did not have souls, that they were not quite human, they were different, they were "no better than animals". . . . The first ghost had begun to walk through dark places in the mind of the South. *Mongrelizing* is a revealing word with connotations of broken taboos and guilt too terrible to say aloud.

These were rural people—rich and poor—many of them

living far away from others of their kind, but close to the animals on farms and plantations, close to this alien race whom
they refused to accept as human, yet they were breeding
with them. Surely something akin to the dread, the anxiety
that is felt by one who indulges in zoophilic practices must
have nagged at their minds on a deep level rarely admitted to
consciousness. What a strange ugly trap the white race made
for itself! Because these slaveholders were "Christian," they
felt compelled to justify the holding of slaves by denying
these slaves a soul, and denying them a place in the human
family. Because they were puritan, they succeeded in developing a frigidity in their white women that precluded the
possibility of mutual satisfaction. Lonely and baffled and
frustrated by the state of affairs they had set up in their own
homes and hearts, they could not resist the vigor and kindliness and gaiety of these slaves. And succumbing to desire,
they mated with these dark women whom they had de-
humanized in their minds, and fathered by them children
who, according to their race philosophy, were "without
souls"—a strange exotic new kind of creature, whom they
made slaves of and sometimes sold on the auction block.
The white man's roles as slaveholder and Christian and puritan were exacting far more than the strength of his mind
could sustain. Each time he found the back-yard temptation
irresistible, his conscience split more deeply from his acts
and his mind from things as they are.

The race-sex-sin spiral had begun. The more trails the
white man made to back-yard cabins, the higher he raised
his white wife on her pedestal when he returned to the big
house. The higher the pedestal, the less he enjoyed her whom
he had put there, for statues after all are only nice things to
look at. More and more numerous became the little trails of
escape from the statuary and more and more intricately they

began to weave in and out of southern life. Guilt, shame, fear, lust spiralled each other. Then a time came, though it was decades later, when man's suspicion of white woman began to pull the spiral higher and higher. It was of course inevitable for him to suspect her of the sins he had committed so pleasantly and often. *What if,* he whispered, and the words were never finished. *What if* . . . . Too often white woman could only smile bleakly in reply to the unasked question. But white man mistook this empty smile for one of cryptic satisfaction and in jealous panic began to project his own sins on to the Negro male. And when he did that, a madness seized our people.

It began slowly, like the tide coming in. Fabulous stories began to be whispered of the Negro male's potency. And as white man visited more frequently the cabins in the quarters, and stayed more and more away from the big house, his suspicion grew of his wife left alone there with her embroidery and her thoughts. The more he left his sacred statuary while he sought warmer company, the more possessive became his words about her. "Our women" was a phrase that was said more and more glibly. And as suspicion and guilt grew, as minds became more paranoid, they threatened with death any white woman who dared do what they had done so freely. It is said—I am not certain that it has been proved—that a few white women did cross over the line and paid their penalty and that this penalty of death was dealt them by their own husband or father or brother as the case might be. I still find myself incredulous about this death legend. But, southern authorities like Hodding Carter and the late William Alexander Percy have, even in recent years, emphasized the strength of the taboo against white women mating with Negroes, and the heavy penalties exacted of them, at least by the community, though now-

adays such women are more often banished than killed; it is
the Negro male who receives the death penalty today as a
"rapist" when such alliances are discovered. Perhaps only in
the Mississippi delta do people still talk in such archaisms
as "our women" and "men's honor," but there was a time
when the South's vocabulary was heavy with such words
and memories even yet are weighed down by them.

Men hungry for political and economic power could not
resist exploiting this terrifying complex of guilt, anxiety, sex
jealousy, and loneliness. By pumping from this vast reservoir
—which had accumulated during long periods of stress—the
mass hysteria they needed to irrigate their political and economic crops, they kept them green. And they are still green
today, cultivated by the same system. It worked so well because the church and the home kept guilt and hate flowing
into the reservoir, while the politician and business man had
nothing to do but keep pumping it out. From this shocking
partnership sprang other crops too, like the Ku Klux Klan
and lynchings, and the massive anxieties which hardened
into the rites of segregation.

If one had tried to dramatize the inward suspicion and
guilt and fear that still gnaws on the white southerner's mind,
it could not have been done more vividly than the Ku Klux
Klan has done it for us. Pictorially, the Klan presents this
Return of the Repressed in a stunning manner. White pillow
case and sheet . . . the face covered . . . identity disap-
pears and with it the conscience . . . a group stalks in silence through the "darkness" . . . a sudden abrupt appear-
ance before the victim . . . and finally, the symbolic killing
of a black male who, according to this paranoid fantasy, has
"raped" a "sacred" white woman. It is a complete acting out
of the white man's internal guilt and his hatred of colored
man and white woman.

Historically, the first Ku Klux Klan originated in Pulaski, Tennessee, in 1866, formed by six ex-Confederate soldiers, half as a lark but used quickly afterward as an impromptu way of meeting an emergency situation in which the South was left without law-enforcing agencies. Had it actually been impromptu and accidental the idea would have been discarded and forgotten when order was restored in the South. But instead, it lived on and spread like an epidemic. Now today, more than eighty years later, the Klan rides in New Jersey as well as in Georgia and Alabama. It no longer limits itself to the revenging of "raping" and the "protecting" of womanhood nor is it turned solely against the Negro race. It is used against unions, against middle-class "deviationists," against people who "drink," against anyone who says or does anything the Klan disapproves of. It is becoming more undisguised and more undifferentiated in its sadism and intolerance, until now it is in the main a ceremonial acting-out of men's deeply repressed fantasies and deeply repressed needs for revenge and penance. It gathers under its hood the mentally ill, the haters who have forgot what it is they hate or who dare not harm their real hate object, and also the bored and confused and ignorant. The Klan is made up of ghosts on the search for ghosts who have haunted the southern soul too long.

There are no available statistics on the frequency or range of biracial sex activities in the South. One has to rely on spotty bits of research, on case studies of southern mental patients, on whispers, and word-of-mouth revelations that go down in the South from white mother to white daughter and from colored mother to colored daughter, and on the garrulous reminiscence of white-haired colonels too old to care, and on the revealing but fragmentary research made by a few social scientists.

Regardless of statistics, this every one knows: Whenever, wherever, race relations are discussed in the United States, sex moves arm in arm with the concept of segregation. There is a union in minds, however unreal in terms of today's facts, that makes us know that the secret history of race relations in the South, the fears and the dreads, are tied up with the secret habits of southerners. We know too, that there are more than six million people of mixed Negro-white blood in our country and most of us are fairly certain that the stork did not bring them to little cotton field cabins—even though in 1940 a Georgia governor banned from state libraries a little book for children written by Dr. Karl de Schweinitz that tells where babies come from.

And now we are close to our second ghost story, which concerns the South's rejected children. When children came from these secret unions they were rarely acknowledged by their white fathers. Usually they were wholly rejected, though now and then they were secretly clung to. Most of us know stories of a white man in our community who chose not to reject his mixed children but educated them instead and helped them find a decent life for themselves. Sometimes he left these children's names in his will and posthumously made amends for human relations which in life he had not the courage to honor. This is one of the brighter threads weaving through the dark evil design of the history of the intimate life of the two races.

But these acknowledgments, though important to remember, have been few. The stark ugly fact is that millions of children have been rejected by their white fathers and white kin and left to battle alone the giants that stalk our culture. Little ghosts playing and laughing and weeping on the edge of the southern memory can be a haunting thing. Surely one can reject a child one has brought into the world only by rejecting an equal part of one's psychic life, putting a sign over it and declaring it does not exist. White and Colored signs have had many uses down here.

This mass rejection of children has been a heavy thing on our region's conscience. Like a dead weight dropped in water it lies deep in the ooze of the old and forgotten, but when talk of change is heard, it stirs restlessly as if still alive in its hiding place and is felt by minds innocent of participating in the original sin but who for involved reasons have identified themselves with it.

The Communists of course have their explanation of this widespread miscegenation. They say it took place in the South because the white man wanted more and more slaves and made of slave women highly profitable economic projects in which he invested spermatozoa. These theorists do not even smile as they spin this odd little yarn. Indeed, to them, there is nothing amusing about it. It is simply a "logical" variation of the twentieth-century Story of Creation in which, according to Marxists, economics is the stork that brings all things, good and bad, to this earth. Since most of us know people to whom money and economic power have come to mean more than love and family and integrity and truth, it is not impossible to believe (though our sense of humor still finds it awkward) that money lust and not body lust drove a few planters deliberately to add to their material wealth in this shrewd, highly pleasurable, if sadistic manner. But the theory will impress most of us as more of an anal-erotic daydream than a rational explanation of group behavior.

But regardless of "why," the results are well known. The men who deviated in this extralegal way were fearful lest their sons, and especially their daughters, should feel the same attraction they felt and should perhaps continue the blending of races to which they and their forefathers had made such lavish contributions. And because they feared this, knowing the strength of temptation, they blocked their children's way by erecting as many barriers as possible, extracting energy from their own guilt to build fortifications of law and custom against what they considered an "irresistible sin." Out of their confusion came that obscene word *mongrelizing* and the sadistic phrase *enforced intimate relations,* both of which were only mirrors of their own shabby past. Like all criminals, they felt compelled to confess their misdeeds and did so almost with the naïveté of a child by the use of these words. Now today's politicians deliberately reach for these worn-out phrases when they need them to stir up excitement and fear and fantasies. Like the South's revivalists, whose place they have in large part taken in communal affairs, these politicians plunge deep into men's minds and memories, and mixing the poison of these words with the guilt already there, they produce terror—and votes.

It is all so foolish and unreal that our sense of humor and our sanity should be able to throw it off. We know conditions have changed. There are still a few casual sex relations between the races, especially in remote rural regions like the delta and in the vicinity of a few of our southern universities, but the old life in the South that bred such deep attraction is almost gone. The back-yard temptation to the front-yard puritan has disappeared, largely due to the fact that so many Negroes have become puritans themselves and back yards are farther away. The patterns of our life have changed rapidly during the last thirty years from rural to urban because of migrations and paved roads. There are fewer personal contacts between the races. There is now in the younger generation a freer and perhaps more rational sex life between male and female of the white group and less necessity to seek pleasure down the back paths. And there is a burning blasting scorn of white men steadily growing in the minds not only of upper-class Negro women but of nearly every woman of the colored race, making it a fairly dangerous thing for any white male to approach one of them.

Yet in spite of these vast changes the old legend persists, sustained by a stubborn memory of a now-lost life. To understand this resurgence of wistful fantasy I think we have to remember that there was more to many of these old affairs than a passing desire for exotic experience or animal lust. Our unwritten history is full of profoundly passionate affairs, of relationships tender and rich and absorbing a lifetime. There were love affairs that made white women despair as competitors; delicate, sensitive, deep relationships in which mind and body and fantasy met in complete union. These have existed and it would make our southern past an impoverished thing were we to try to erase them because of the puritanic pride of either of the two races.

They existed because there was rich psychological soil for them to grow in. In the old days, a white child who had loved his colored nurse, his "mammy" with that passionate devotion which only small children feel, who had grown used to dark velvety skin, warm deep breast, rich soothing voice and the ease of a personality whose religion was centered in heaven not hell, who had felt when mind is tender the touch of a spirit almost free of sex anxiety, found it natural to seek in adolescence and adulthood a return of this profoundly pleasing experience. His memory was full of echoes . . . he could not rid himself of them. And he followed these echoes to back-yard cabins, to colored town, hoping to find there the substance of shadowy memories. Sometimes he found what he sought and formed a tender and passionate and deeply satisfying relation which he was often faithful to, despite cultural barriers. But always it was a relationship without honor in his own mind and region, and the source of profound anxiety which seeped like poison through his personality. Yet with it was always the old longing, the old desire for something that he could not find in his white life.

Stifled, sometimes forced into the unconscious, though betrayed ingenuously by the bathos of the "my old mammy" theme, this ambivalent and tragic relationship of childhood —the white child and his colored nurse—has powerfully influenced the character of many southerners of the dominant class. The class is small, numerically, but out of it have come politicians, newspaper editors and journalists, college professors and presidents, doctors, preachers, industrialists, bankers, writers, governors, and their wives, and in our national government many of the prominent officials who are today determining the future of the world. It therefore seems important for us to understand this primal experience which so many leaders in world affairs and designers of American opinion have undergone in childhood.

It was customary in the South, if a family possessed a moderate income, to have a colored nurse for the children. Sometimes such a one came with the first child and lived in the family until the last one was grown. Her role in the family was involved and of tangled contradictions. She always knew her "place," but neither she nor her employers could have defined it. She was given a limited authority, but it was elastic enough to stretch into dictatorship over not only children but the white mother and sometimes even the male head of the family. They leaned on her strength because they had so little of their own, or because she had so much, and once leaning they could not free themselves from subjection. Many an old nurse, knowing all there was to know of her white folks, familiar with every bone of every skeleton in their closets, gradually became so dominating that her employers actually feared her power. Yet she was a necessary part of these big sprawling households; her knowledge, alone, of how to grow children was too precious a thing to throw away lightly, and her value extended far beyond child rearing. She nursed old and young when they were sick, counseled them when they were unhappy, took the problem child at least out of earshot, and in crises her biologically-rooted humor had a magic way of sweeping white clouds away. She was nurse, witch doctor, and priest, conjuring off our warts, our hurt feelings and stomach-aches, all of which disappeared when she said they would. She knew wonderful simples for ailments of body and soul, and bound up both in earthy ointments. We put on undershirts, come fall, as she told us to, hung asafetida bags around our necks when there were epidemics in town, ate sulphur and cream of tartar each spring, stayed away from graveyards after dark as she taught us to do, wouldn't have dared iron anything on Sunday, and following her precepts we prospered as did her own children. Sometimes Mr. White Man himself did not deem it beneath him to call on her for help. "Mammy, come in here and talk to Miss Sarah [his wife]. Talk sense to her, Mammy," and he'd leave for the cotton gin downtown or the sawmill hoping to God that Mammy could straighten Sarah out. And usually she did, and Sarah would be as meek and gentle as a wife should be when her husband returned that evening.

In many homes, the nurse was also a wet nurse. We were children in the pre-refrigerator age and bottle feeding was a perilous business. It was much safer when mother's milk disagreed, to turn an ailing or malnourished infant over to a nurse whose ample breasts could take care of another as

well as her own. It was not a rare sight in my generation to
see a black woman with a dark baby at one breast and a
white one at the other, rocking them both in her wide lap,
shushing them to sleep as she hummed her old songs. Still
swinging them from side to side in her arms, she would lay
them down on the same pallet underneath a shade tree and
leave them there, little black little white together, sleeping
in peace. These intimacies fill our memories and do strange
things now to our segregated grown-up lives.

In my home, our nurse lived in the back yard beyond
Mother's flower garden in a small cabin whose interior walls
were papered with newspapers. Much of my very young life
was spent there. I was turned over to her when a new baby
took my place in the family. And because I seemed not to
have the stamina to adjust to this little intruder I protested
by refusing to eat and kept up a food strike so long that they
grew alarmed and called in the doctor although Aunt Chloe
looked on, they say, with obvious scorn at their panic. And
after the doctor left his prescription and drove away in his
buggy, she took me to her cabin and kept me there. The
story is that Aunt Chloe tried food after food all of which
I rejected, then studying the pale young face before her for
a little, she suddenly took a little food, chewed it first in her
mouth, put it in mine and I swallowed it promptly. Soon I
was prospering on this fine psychological diet, gaining in
weight and security as the weeks went by. I was once more
the center of somebody's universe. What did it matter that
this universe encompassed only one room in a little back-
yard cabin? It filled my need and I loved her.

Such a relationship with such a woman is not to be brushed
off by the semantic trick of labelling her a "nurse."

Sometimes these nurses took over the care of a baby on
the day it was born. More often Mammy entered a child's

life in an important way at the painful moment when a new baby had taken its place. Wounded and hurt, feeling as profound a rejection as the human heart knows, we were taken into her life, where she made us feel welcome and prized. In her own way and not wholly according to what the psychiatrists of today would suggest, she helped us adjust to the one who had taken our place, nursed us through and sometimes, not always, weaned us from this experience that grasped like nettles and threatened to hold us to it for the rest of our lives. But though freed from this, we were tied fast to another, even more difficult, relationship.

Psychoanalysts have made us know during the past decades how the deep injuries to the infant psyche can leave scar tissue that binds a personality for a lifetime. We have grown used to words we do not always understand: the Oedipus complex, "fixation," and the pictures of rejection that haunt the child memory. But this dual relationship which so many white southerners have had with two mothers, one white and one colored and each of a different culture that centered in different human values, makes the Oedipus complex seem by comparison almost a simple adjustment.

Before the ego had gained strength, just as he is reaching out to make his first ties with the human family, this small white child learns to love both mother and nurse; he is never certain which he loves better. Sometimes, secretly, it is his "colored mother" who meets his infantile needs more completely, for his "white mother" is busy with her social life or her older children or perhaps a new one, and cannot give him the time and concern he hungers for. Yet before he knows words, he dimly perceives that his white mother has priority over his colored mother, that somehow he "belongs" more to her, though he may stay more with the other. But he is satisfied with things as they are, for his colored mother meets his immediate needs as he hungers to have them met. She is easy, permissive, less afraid of simple earthy biological needs and manifestations. When naughtiness must be punished, it is not hers but the white mother's prerogative to do so; and afterward, little white child runs back to colored mother for comfort and sugar-tits. Sometimes, white child hates white mother after this ordeal, and clings desperately to his colored mother, who soothes him and gives him a tea cake as she softly asks him, "Ain' you shamed, honey, to be so bad!" And he is shamed, and confused, and sometimes very lonely also.

And now curious things happen. Strong bonds begin to grow as the most profound relationships of his life are formed, holding him to two women whose paths will take them far from each other. It is as if he were fastened to two umbilical cords which wrap themselves together in a terrifying tangle, and then suddenly, inexplicably, but with awful sureness, begin steadily to move, each in a different direction. Because white mother has always set up right and wrong, has with authority established the "do" and the "don't" of behavior, his conscience, as it grows in him, ties its allegiance to her and to the white culture and authority which she and his father represent. But to colored mother, persuasive in her relaxed attitude toward "sin," easy and warm in her physical ministrations, generous with her petting, he ties his pleasure feelings.

Big white house, little cabin, enter the picture he is slowly forming in his mind about this strange world he lives in, and both begin subtly to give pattern to it. A profound separation has begun, a crack that extends deep into his personality. He erects "white" image-ideals and secretly pulls them down again. He says aloud what his heart denies stubbornly. Part of him stays more and more in the world he "belongs" in; part of him stays forever in the world he dare not acknowledge. He feels deep tenderness for his colored nurse and pleasure in being with her, but he begins to admire more and more the lovely lady who is his "real" mother. He is impressed by her white beauty, her clothes and grace and charm; he feels one with the big powerful man who is his father—though he fears him too and sometimes secretly hates him—and one with the tradition that stands like the big house he was born in, always there before him as "his." But when he is miserable, he creeps away and crawls up in old black arms, every curve of which he has known by heart since babyhood, and snuggles against a cotton dress that is ragged maybe but will always smell good to his memory. . . . Sometimes he wants to stay in her lap forever; but he slips away shamefaced, remembering that his mother is not "fitten," as she says herself, to sit in the living room and eat at the table with the rest of the family. He is learning a bitter, desolating lesson that shrinks the heart when we think of its human implications; and soon he will know it too well ever to forget it.

His "white" conscience, now, is hacking at his early love life, splitting it off more and more sharply into acceptable and unacceptable, what is done and what isn't; into "pure" and "impure"; Madonna and whore; Mother and nurse; wife and prostitute; white conscience and colored pleasures; marriage and lust; "right" and "wrong"; belief and act; segregation and brotherhood. He accords his mother the esteem and respect that are hers; he feels more and more a pulling obligation to her, though he does not know why. And after a time, he feels that he "owes" her so much that he steals the adoration which he had conferred upon his colored mother long ago, and returns it to his white mother as rightfully hers. From now on, his gifts to his old nurse will be little presents, not of esteem and love, but a linen handkerchief or a check at Christmas and birthday, and all his life long, tears when old spirituals are sung. . . .

He has almost completed the cheapening of this tender profound relationship that his culture insists upon. The segregation of his first love feelings is nearly perfected, but not quite; not ever is it quite finished. Deep down in him, he often reserves his play, his "real" pleasure, his relaxed enjoyment of sex activities, and his fantasy, for women as much like his nurse (they may or may not have colored skin) as his later life can discover. Now he has achieved his stature as a white man; he has accepted the life that his color conferred upon him. But he is never at ease. The deep powerful drives of childhood will not stay in the little stream beds his culture gullied out for them. Again and again they overflow, sweeping across him like a flood. Tenderness for his mother turns into sudden cruelty for his wife which he conceals even from himself sometimes, or betrays by lightning flashes of hatred. Sometimes he loses the shame he is trained to feel about women of other color or class and admits to himself and to others his pleasure in them. Sometimes a sweeping sadistic feeling for all women overpowers him. He feels betrayed, cheated; and he despises himself and them for a treacherous partnership in which he seems always to have been the loser since childhood. And in deep repugnance, he sometimes turns away from all women, shunning them white and black, and spends his real feelings on men and his hours in companionship with them, or centers his energy on making money, more and more money.

However they dealt with it, nearly all men—and women— of the dominant class in the South suffered not only the usual painful experiences of growing up in America but this special southern trauma in which segregation not only divided the races but divided the white child's heart.

Three ghost relationships—white man and colored woman, white father and colored children, white child and his beloved colored nurse—haunting the mind of the South and giving shape to our lives and our souls.

And there was a fourth, poisoned by disesteem as were the others, yet a relationship that held the good qualities of one person firmly to the good of another. Back-yard though it was, lopsided by color, curiously belittled by those who valued it most, this friendship between individuals of the two races was a thing of kindliness and mutual concern. Begun in childhood, it sometimes was broken only by death. Shamefaced though they were in its presence, men white and colored sacrificed themselves sometimes in its name. This friendship across barriers has been, of all bi-racial relationships in the South, the one most enriching in its human qualities; and one that has often restrained the region from insane excesses of prejudice. It nourished no guilt, sheltered no hate, was not used as an escape from responsibilities. It was no ghost, but a real thing that bound men one to another though there was between them a deep chasm that drained away much that is good from the lives of both. There was no honor in that relationship but there was a secret acceptance of each other as human. And it became a green growing thing in that desert which disesteem and lack of responsibility had made of the southerner's human relations.

I remember, as a child, the bitterness on faces of my father's and grandfather's friends and other men on Main Street in the little town where I was reared. Quick, hearty laughter and so few warm smiles. . . . I remember the easy tears in hard old eyes and unhappy lips and weathered faces, reddened by sun in the sensitive way of Scotch-Irish skins. I remember mouths moving restlessly, chewing tobacco, smoking a pipe, munching a straw, or cursing, or saying low words to other men as eyes lingered on hard young female buttocks sashaying down bright streets. There would be laughter, mirthless, oozing uncleanliness. And then the old men would turn, and seeing little school children watching them gravely, they would in the way of grown-ups give them a stick of candy from the store counter or hand them a nickel and tell them to buy themselves a cold drink or a package of chewing gum. . . .

Those faces on Main Street shaded by wide straw hats are surrounded in my child-memory by hardware and ploughs, seed bags and bales of cotton, the smell of guano and mule lots, hot sun on sidewalks and lovely white ladies with sweet childlike voices and smooth, childlike faces, and old gardens of boxwood and camellias, and fields endlessly curving around my small world. I know now that the bitterness, the cruel sensual lips, the quick tears in hard eyes, the sashaying buttocks of brown girls, the thin childish voices of white women, had a great deal to do with high interest at the bank and low wages in the mills and gullied fields and lynchings and Ku Klux Klan and segregation and sacred womanhood and revivals, and Prohibition. And that no part of this memory can be understood without recalling all of it.

There were other faces, and I remember them also—in church, office, library, or school, or newspaper office. Tired faces, often, and of a slow charm, and gentle, with voice soft-spoken and of profound hesitation, or sometimes urbane and witty. These were the faces you saw of men who feared the "outbreak of violence," who wrote editorials suggesting things must change slowly, who read poetry or wrote it, who said, "You can't turn the South upside down overnight," who said, "Whatever is done for the Negro—and things should be done—must be done under the system of segregation we have lived under all of our lives." These faces belonged to men loyal to their "white mothers" and loyal in a secret, deep-rooted way, to their dark ones also; loyal above all else to the conscience their mothers gave them, men who clung to their white culture as a cripple clings to his crutches; whose passion and memories had been deeply repressed, and who had put up signs long ago in their unconscious and had forbidden themselves ever to trespass them.

Tired liberals. Remembering them now and my own generation's fatigue, I find myself wondering if Mammy in Dixie and Nanny in England have ever been given their due credit for the rise of Anglo-Saxon liberalism—not only in its tortured form but in its best manifestations of moderation and justice and mercy and value of human life.

There were those also, who could neither successfully repress their feelings nor give outlet to them; whose minds and hearts, whose hate and love were in never-ceasing combat that drained all strength away: our small-town failures from the best families . . . and some of the most charming men on earth.

And there were the few who were different, who somehow found a center around which to build their lives and their region. These gave us our strength, held us back from too much self-pity, reached out for the new, made great errors and achieved real triumphs. There were not many, but our region cannot forget them for they were those who carried out their beliefs, limited as these beliefs were, and refused to bow down to confusion.

But even these men did not see what segregation had done to the South's women, pushed away on that lonely pedestal called Sacred Womanhood.

⌒ 4 ⌒

The Women

OF ALL the painful and humiliating experiences which southern white women endured, the least easy to accept, I think, was that of a mother who had no choice but to take the husk of a love which her son in his earliest years had given to another woman. She valiantly made jokes about it, telling her friends that her child preferred Mammy to her and that was fine, wasn't it, for it gave her so much more time to attend to all she had to do! "I don't know how I could have done without her," she would say and laugh a light tinkling laugh which sounded like little glass bells about to break into splinters. "Mammy was wonderful," she'd say. "I just don't see how we could do without the colored folks, do you?" she'd say. "I declare! but aren't the younger ones trifling—now look at that Emmy, doing nothing but rolling a dip stick around in her mouth and humming and with her shoes off again! But when I hear men say, 'Send 'em all back to Africa,' I say *they* don't have the housework to do, why we couldn't possibly . . . Oh, my!" sighing and laughing, and trying to forget things she could never forget.

This giving up of one's men and one's childhood to colored

women—for the girl-child was shaped as subtly as little
boys by the nurse-mother relationship—took on the unreal,
shadowy quality of a dream; a recurring dream that southern white women could not rid themselves of. One's self
. . . one's father . . . one's husband . . . one's son. . . .
Sometimes in the old days it made a pattern like that: a
stark dance that all their life long they tread the bleak
measures of, with heart too heavy and body too rigid to
make of space anything but a thin line to hold to on the way
to a death that would not come soon enough.

A secret wound that can never be spoken aloud or shown
is not tragedy for tragedy finds its stature on a stage where
it can feel beyond it, its audience. To these women their life
was only a shameful sore that could not be acknowledged
because of its origin in sin.

Sometimes they could weep. A soundless weeping that
trickled down into the crevices of personality leaving damp
little places for thorns to grow, and sometimes for pale
ghostly flowers that gave a fragrance of death to certain
women. You remember these women from your childhood,
and as you remember you keep thinking of old lost graveyards under oak trees where moss swings in the still air as
if to the heartbeat of the dead, and small carved lambs
watch over baby mounds; you keep thinking of cape jasmine
in your mother's back yard, and the way you felt in the night
when you awoke after dreams and smelled the night-bloom-
ing cereus below the window. . . .

It was as if these women never quite left the presence of
the dead but mourned gently and continuously a loss that
they could not bear to know the extent of. Unable to look
at the ugly facts of their own life, they learned to see mysterious things the rest of us could never see. I remember
how they "felt" premonitions, counting shadows and making
of them cryptic answers. They "dreamed" that a beloved

one would die and the beloved sometimes died! They "felt" there would be no returning when one left on a long journey and sometimes there was no return! They chanted so sweetly the death-knell of those they loved that I remember how carefully I avoided these friends of my mother's who dwelt serenely among disasters, for I feared that one day a gentle Cassandra might hold the syllables of my name on her tongue.

The little ghost women of small southern towns . . . swishing softly into church, sometimes singing in the choir, slipping like their carefully made custards down the dark maw of life. Their number was few. One remembers them because they roam even now so restlessly through time. I think, however, that most women of my mother's age, though their characters were twisted and shaped by these troubles, retained a more earthy quality and sometimes a firm grasp indeed on things of this world. The pain they felt they denied or tried to displace. Surely this emptiness was the natural way women should feel! Like childbirth pangs and menstrual cramps, the sexual erosion of their nature was "God's way" and hence if you were sensible must be accepted. But some stubbornly called it "female trouble" and went to doctors' offices as often as to church, to moan their misery.

A few "solved it all" by rejecting their womanly qualities. They seemed to hate and envy men for their freedom from pain and their access to pleasure. And sometimes they hated their own Maker too (a blasphemy they carefully hid from their minds) for giving females the long agony of parturition and none of the male's quick ecstasy of procreation. Yet there was usually a curious loyalty to their own father, though every other man was not "fit to be lived with." In later decades, when women were freer, these protesters turned toward the cities, gathering together, a grim little number, cropping their hair short, walking in heavy awk-ward strides, and acquiring, as do subjugated people every-where when protesting their chains, the more unpleasant qualities of this enemy who had segregated them from their birthright. Not daring in the secret places of their minds to confess what they really wanted, they demanded to be treated "exactly like men." They were of course a part of the psychosexual, economic, political protest of women arising throughout Western culture, a kind of fibroid growth of sick cells multiplying aggressiveness in an attempt at cure. But there was no comfortable place for such women in the South, though a few of these rebels lived in every town.

The majority of southern women convinced themselves that God had ordained that they be deprived of pleasure, and meekly stuffed their hollowness with piety, trying to believe that the tightness they felt was hunger satisfied. Culturally stunted by a region that still pays nice rewards to simple-mindedness in females, they had no defenses against blandishment. They listened to the round words of men's tribute to Sacred Womanhood and believed, thinking no doubt that if they were not sacred then what under God's heaven *was* the matter with them! Once hoisted up by the old colonels' oratory, they stayed on lonely pedestals and rigidly played "statue" while their men went about more important affairs elsewhere.

These women turned away from the ugliness which they felt powerless to cope with and made for themselves and their families what they called a "normal" life. Their homes, often simple, were gracious and good to live in. The South—if one can forget the shabby milltowns, the rickety Colored Towns, the surrealist city tenements—is full of such homes. Places you remember—if you live on that side of town—of quiet ease and comfort and taste. In these homes, food and flowers were cherished, and old furniture, and the family's past (screened of all but the pleasing and the trivial). Sex was pushed out through the back door as a shameful thing never to be mentioned. Segregation was pushed out of sight also, and this was managed so successfully that until the last twenty years, most white southerners cheerfully said there was no race problem for it had been "solved." Out through the back door went the unpleasant and unmentionable; in through the back door came trays laden with food as delicious as can be found in the world. Though asceticism controlled the regions left out of the physiology books, and Prohibition succeeded sometimes in banishing the bottle, the groaning table was left free.

Whatever the hurt in our lives, there are these memories of food, and flowers, and of southern gardens, filled with our mothers' fantasies that had no other way to creep into life. Ladies and their garden clubs have been made by cartoonists into a national laugh, and sometimes a funny one, but some of us can smile for only a moment. We are always remembering a face we love and the longing in it as plants were set in damp ground and shaded against the sun. . . . A figure stooping, familiar hands feeling around in warm soft dirt to slip a weed out, planting and transplanting little secret dreams, making them live in an azalea, a rose, a camellia, when they could not live in their own arid lives. . . . A voice grown plaintive over a peaked little plant that refused to bloom . . . so softly scolding the flowers for not living their life to its full. In the mornings these old gardens full of lively bugs, and toads hopping among the violets, and new blow-y spider webs that never break in the memory, were like a clear mind filled with bright dewy ideas. But at night in the moonlight, a woman walking alone, up and down prim rows of camellias or in summer among the lilies, even now can make one want to close the gates against the past forever—so hurting is the realization of an anguish that need not have been.

With their gardens and their homes, these women tried to shut out evil, and sometimes succeeded in sheltering their children from it. If you could only keep from them the things of our South that must never be mentioned, all would be well! Innocence, virtue, ignorance, silence were synonyms twining around young lives like smilax. It was not evil but the knowledge of it that injured, these mothers believed. What you don't hear or read or see surely can never be known to you. And because they did not believe things *could* change or that they should change (though they could not have told you why) they had to shut their own minds against knowledge of evil also. They could not let their imaginations feel the sorrow of a colored mother whose child is shamed from birth, nor once look deep into poverty, nor once touch the agony of a back-door life lived forever and ever, nor once realize what they themselves had been deprived of. They could not have borne it. And because they could not let themselves know, they were terrified at a word, a suggestion, anything that caused them to feel deeply. It was as if one question asked aloud might, like a bulldozer, uproot their garden of fantasies and tear it in a few moments out of time, leaving only naked bleeding reality to live with.

There were others whose minds perhaps were not brighter, but whose natures could not accept life so meekly. They felt compelled to question and to answer their own questions. They would not have used the word "sex" aloud, but their questions and answers told them that all a woman can expect from lingering on exalted heights is a hard chill afterward; that indeed, white women had not profited in the least from the psychosexual profit system which segregation in the South supported so lavishly; and that furthermore, no

bargain had been made with them in any of these trans-
actions. They learned that *discrimination* was a word with
secret meanings and they did not like its secrets. This much
of semantics they understood as clearly as their recipe for
beaten biscuits. In the white southern woman's dictionary,
discrimination could be defined as a painful way of life
which too often left an empty place in her bed and an ache
in the heart. Whether or not these women had themselves
experienced this pain—and we must remember that many
had not—they knew segregation in the South had cleaved
through white woman's tenderest dreams. They had seen it
turn a woman's life drama of child, wife, mother into tragedy, or more often into plain vulgar melodrama. How could
they sit in the audience and applaud their own humilia-
tion?

So, learning these answers to their questions, they climbed
down from the pedestal when no one was looking and explored a bit. Not as you may think, perhaps. They were con-
ventional, old-fashioned, highly "moral" women, who would
not have dreamed of breaking the letter of their marriage
vows or, when not married, their technical chastity. But
their minds went a-roaming and their sympathies attached
themselves like hungry little fibers to all kinds of people and
causes while their shrewd common sense kicked old lies
around until they were popping like firecrackers.

These ladies went forth to commit treason against a southern tradition set up by men who had betrayed their mothers,
sometimes themselves, and many of the South's children
white and mixed, for three long centuries. It was truly a
subversive affair, but as decorously conducted as an afternoon walk taken by the students of a Female Institute. It
started stealthily, in my mother's day. Shyly, these first
women sneaked down from their chilly places, did their
little sabotage and sneaked up again, wrapping innocence

around them like a lace shawl. They set secret time bombs and went back to their needlework, serenely awaiting the blast. They had no lady Lincoln to proclaim their emancipation from southern tradition but they scarcely needed one.

The thing was a spontaneous reaction. Mother in her old age told daughter strange truths that had gnawed on her lonely heart too long. And daughter told other women. Colored and white women stirring up a lemon-cheese cake for the hungry males in the household looked deep into each other's eyes and understood their common past. A mistress, reading the Bible to her colored maid polishing silver, would lay aside Holy Writ and talk of things less holy but of immense importance to both of them.

Insurrection was on. White men were still unaware of it, but the old pedestal on which for so long their women had been safely stowed away, was reeling and rocking. With an emotionally induced stupidity really beneath them, these men went on with their race-economic exploitation, protecting themselves behind rusty shields of as phony a moral cause as the Anglo-American world has ever witnessed. In the name of *sacred womanhood*, of *purity*, of *preserving the home*, lecherous old men and young ones, reeking with impurities, who had violated the home since they were sixteen years old, whipped up lynchings, organized Klans, burned crosses, aroused the poor and ignorant to wild excitement by an obscene, perverse imagery describing the "menace" of Negro men hiding behind every cypress waiting to rape "our" women. In the name of such holiness, they did these things to keep the affairs of their own heart and conscience and home, as well as the community, "under control." And not once did they dream that their women did not believe their lies.

And then it happened. The lady insurrectionists gathered together in one of our southern cities. They primly called

themselves church women but churches were forgotten by
everybody when they spoke their revolutionary words. They
said calmly that they were not afraid of being raped; as for
their sacredness, they could take care of it themselves; they
did not need the chivalry of a lynching to protect them and
did not want it. Not only that, they continued, but they
would personally do everything in their power to keep any
Negro from being lynched and furthermore, they squeaked
bravely, they had plenty of power.

They had more than they knew. They had the power of
spiritual blackmail over a large part of the white South. All
they had to do was to drop their little bucket into any one of
numerous wells of guilt dotting the landscape and splash
it around a bit. No one, of thousands of white men, had any
notion how much or how little each woman knew about his
private goings-on. Some who had never been guilty in act
began to equate adolescent fantasies with reality, and there
was confusion everywhere.

This was in 1930. These women organized an Association
of Southern Women for the Prevention of Lynching. Their
husbands, sons, brothers, and uncles often worked proudly
by their side; many of them with sincere concern for the state
of affairs, others because they had to.

Though it may seem incredible to all but southerners, the
custom of lynching had so rarely been questioned that these
church women's action gave a genuine shock. For this was
a new thing in Dixie. The ladies' valor is not diminished, I
think, by reminding ourselves that the movement could not
have crystallized so early had not Dr. Will Alexander, and
a handful of men and women whom he gathered around
him, pushed things off to a good start in 1918 with the first
interracial committee in the South. There were other yeasty
forces at work: A world war had squeezed and pulled the
earth's people apart and squeezed them together again; the

Negroes themselves, led by courageous men like Walter White of Atlanta and W. E. B. Du Bois and their northern white friends were making our nation aware that Negroes have rights; the group around Dr. Howard Odum—whose first study of the Negro in 1910 greatly influenced social science's interest in Negro-white patterns of life—were gathering all kinds of facts concerning a region that had been for so long content with its fantasies and fears. The women's role was to bake the first pan of bread made from this rising batter, and to serve it hot as is southern custom.

After this magnificent uprising against the sleazy thing called "chivalry," these women worked like the neat, industrious housewives they really were, using their mops and brooms to clean up a dirty spot here and there but with no real attempt to change this way of life which they dimly realized had injured themselves and their children as much as it had injured Negroes, but which they nevertheless clung to.

Of course the demagogues would have loved to call them "Communists" or "bolsheviks," but how could they? The women were too prim and neat and sweet and ladylike and churchly in their activities, and too many of them were the wives of the most powerful men in town. Indeed, the ladies themselves hated the word "radical" and were quick to turn against anyone who dared go further than they in this house-cleaning of Dixie. Few of them had disciplined intellects or giant imaginations and probably no one of them grasped the full implications of this sex-race-religion-economics tangle, but they had warm hearts and powerful energy and a nice technic for bargaining, and many an old cagey politician, and a young one or two, have been outwitted by their soft bending words.

They followed a sound feminine intuition, working as "church women," leaning on the strength of Christ's teachings for support when they needed it. They worked with great bravery but so unobtrusively that even today many southerners know little about them. But they aroused the conscience of the South and the whole country about lynching; they tore a big piece of this evil out of southern tradition, leaving a hole which no sane man in Dixie now dares stuff up with public defenses. They attacked the KKK when few except Julian Harris of the Columbus (Georgia) *Enquirer*, among white southern newspaper men, had criticized this group from whom Hitler surely learned so much. And they have continued this fight (known to demagogues as "northern meddling"), joining their energies with other church women throughout the nation.

But they were not yet done. They had a few more spots to rub out. One had to do with their own souls. They believed that the Lord's Supper is a holy sacrament which Christians cannot take without sacrilege unless they will also break bread with fellow men of other color. Believing, they put on their best bib and tucker and gathered in small groups to eat with colored women, deliberately breaking a taboo that had collected around it as many deep fears as any in southern culture.

It is sometimes difficult for those not reared as white southerners to remember how this eating taboo in childhood is woven into the mesh of things that are "wrong," how it becomes tangled with God and sex, pulling anxieties from stronger prohibitions and attaching them to itself. But we who live here can never forget. One of these church women told me of her experience when she first ate with colored friends. Though her conscience was serene, and her enjoyment of this association with colored women was real, yet she was seized by an acute nausea which disappeared only when the meal was finished. She was too honest to attribute it to anything other than deep-rooted anxiety welling up from the "bottom of her personality," as she expressed it, creeping back from her childhood training. Others have told me similar experiences: of feeling "pangs of conscience," as one put it, "though my conscience was clearly approving"; or suddenly in the night awaking, overwhelmed by "serious doubts of the wisdom of what we are doing."

The white women were not alone in these irrational reactions. Colored women also found it hard, but for different reasons. Sometimes their pride was deeply hurt that white women felt so virtuous when eating with them. They were too sensitive not to be aware of the psychic price the white women paid for this forbidden act, and yet too ignorant of the training given white children to understand why there had to be a price. And sometimes the colored women were themselves almost overcome by a break-through not of guilt but of their old repressed hatred of white people. One of the most charming, sensitive, intelligent Negro women I know, tells me that even now when she is long with white people she grows physically ill and has immense difficulty coming to terms with the resentments of her childhood.

To break bread together as Christians, each group had to force its way through thick psychological barriers, and each did it with little understanding of their own or the other group's feelings. When the seizures came, most of the church women, white and Negro, suppressed them simply and firmly by laying the ponderous weight of the New Testament on their fears and hurts, declaring bravely that "Jesus would have done likewise."

In more recent years this group, united with the church women in all parts of the nation and from most of our denominations, has taken a stand against segregation in the church. The same group in Atlanta whose nucleus is now under Dorothy Tilly's fine leadership—and supported by the Southern Regional Council—has made during the past year

a brave strong stand against segregation in our higher
schools of learning and in interstate travel. They are daring
more these days, doing fewer paint jobs and more car-
pentry on the old Southern Mansion, adding rooms in it for
the rest of the family. And because they are, they are not receiving the indulgence of newspapers and politicians that
they once had. Perhaps the old power of spiritual blackmail
has waned. Perhaps also, these women are developing new
powers, new technics, and are beginning to be feared in
new ways. However much or little they have accomplished
(and sometimes it seems a small thing set against the size
and urgency of the job), these church women found for
themselves a sublimation of the deprivations that their culture had exacted of their sex and used their freed energy and
love to spread a green-growing cover crop on the South's
worn-out spiritual soil. In that strange and lovely and rare
way of human nature, they pushed aside their own trouble
and somehow grew mature enough to reach out with compassion toward those more miserable. It seemed almost as
if they lifted their natures by their own leverage though
they would say that it was their faith in the teachings of
Jesus that lifted them.

It would be pleasant to stop the story of the South's
women here, but there is a more tragic page.

Like their men, most of these deeply hurt women found
it easier to cultivate hate than love in their natures. Their
own dreams destroyed, they destroyed in cruelty their children's dreams and their men's aspirations.

It was a compulsive thing they did, with no awareness of
the unconscious hate compelling them to do it. Most of
them felt they were doing "right." Most of them thought it
was their duty to watch closely over the morals of their
children and husbands. They did not see themselves in the

ungracious role of exacting of their family the same obedi-
ence to the same Authority that had exacted so much of
them. They thought they loved their husbands and children so much that they wanted them to do "right." They
would have been horrified had they been accused of setting
up their home as a juvenile court and themselves as the
judge, though that is what they too often did.

They would have been more deeply shocked had they
been accused of hate. They felt nothing but love for their
families and sometimes a bit of vexation and disappointment.
They nursed them tenderly through illness, planned delicious
meals for them, kept the home physically pleasant, were
ambitious and proud of their achievements, and felt that
they were utterly devoted wives and mothers. They "sacrificed" all their lives long but they never looked clearly at
what they were sacrificing.

The little thorns growing deep in secret wounds thrust up
sharp points into their conscience, making it a prickly thing,
but they covered it with the soft folds of affectionate concern and hid from themselves the thorn tips. When they
turned this conscience against their children, or the men in
their family, they thought they were doing God's will. And,
as is the tragic way of humans, in the name of "what is
right" they committed as great evil at home as did their
men in the name of Sacred Womanhood over in Colored
Town or at the state capitals, or as nations have done in the
name of freedom in recent mass wars.

Many a man went into politics, or joined the KKK, had a
nervous breakdown or forged checks, got drunk or built up
a great industry, because he could no longer bear the police-
state set up in his own home. But this would have been a
hard thing for these good mothers and wives to believe,
and for the men also.

As time passed, mothers went more and more compulsively about the training of their children as if it were a totalitarian discipline: imposing rigidities on spirit and mind, imposing eating schedules as if eating were a duty, elimination schedules as if elimination were a responsibility one owed to one's state, hurrying weaning as if suckling were an immoral habit that babies must give up as soon as possible, binding the curiosity of childhood as the Chinese once bound their little girls' feet.

More and more rigid became this training and more steellike and impersonal. It was all such a desperate business. If they had been asked what they feared, or to list the evils their children might "find out," they would have been deeply bewildered. They sometimes had tears but no words for their anxiety. They only knew that they must keep their children pure and innocent, they must "make" them good. They felt that inside each little body, inside each mind, there was a powerful force, a kind of atomic energy; if let out, it might blast their children's "morals" to pieces. They were compelled, therefore, to spend their time walling up this danger. With a rigid training they armored their children against their fantasies and sex feelings, preparing them for human relations as if for a cruel medieval battle. Thus they segregated sex from love and tenderness and obligation, and did not see how inevitably it would slip into secret back-door union with hate and guilt.

This training, until recent decades, was often complicated by the child's dual Mother-Mammy relationship. For sometimes Mother would give orders which Mammy, more wise in the ways of childhood, would not carry out. Many a child of my generation was split as deeply in his moral nature as in his first human relationships by a white mother's code that colored nurse intuitively knew was too rigid and unreal for the warm, pliant human spirit to adhere to. Though in many ways it was a thing to be grateful for, sometimes in-

stinctual needs of the body were satisfied at so exorbitant
a price exacted by conscience that the personality could
not pay it.

We cannot let ourselves forget that their culture had
stripped these women of profound biological rights, had
ripped off their inherent dignity and made of them silly
statues and psychic children, stunting their capacity for rich
understanding and enjoyment of husbands and family. It is
not strange that they became vigilant guardians of a southern tradition which in guarding they often, unbeknownst to
their own minds, avenged themselves on with a Medea-like
hatred.

In most of them there was a profound subservience; they
dared not question what had injured them so much. It was
all wrapped up in one package: sex taboos, race segregation,
"the right to make money the way Father made money,"
the duty to go to church, the fear of new knowledge that
would shake old beliefs, the splitting of ideals from actions
—and you accepted it all as uncritically as the Communists
accept their Stalin-stamped lives. And you insisted on others
accepting it also. You dreaded a deviationist, you were in
terror lest your children be other than orthodox southerners.
You used your conscience as if it were a hypodermic needle,
plunging it into the tenderest spots of young spirits, filling
them with your guilt, hoping to inoculate them "for their
own good" against vague, dread "evils."

But it was a tainted needle that spread through these
children a poison that came out in unhealing sores.

It would be as unfair to blame the mothers of two or three
generations for a way of life that began twisting and turning
and destroying its children long before they were born, as
it would be to blame the men. Both men and women were
born into it and of it. And because it is a culture that lacks
almost completely the self-changing power that comes from

honest criticism, because in the past it forced out its children who saw dangers and tried to avert them, who had insight and talents that could have contributed so richly to the South's recovery; because it bruised those who grimly stayed, unwelcomed, until their energies were depleted (we have only to recall Howard Odum's stormy years, and Arthur Raper, H. C. Nixon, William Kilpatrick, and numerous poets, teachers, authors, who were forced into exile or stayed at home under bitter attack)—because it did these things to its own men, it is not difficult to understand why these women, our mothers and perhaps ourselves, could not do other than bend to the system and think it "right" to bend to it. They did not have enough insight—where could they have got it?—to grow wary of a conscience that drives ruthlessly across natural, spontaneous needs. They did not dream that the energy driving this conscience might be hate, not love. They could not have accepted the terrifying fact that their own banned desires had slipped into their conscience giving it its cruel power. They had not questioned life closely enough—for life gave harsh answers to questions —to discover that guilt and ideals are as different sometimes as the insane and the sane.

We cannot censure—who would dare!—but we know now with tragic certainty that these women, forced by their culture and their heartbreak, did a thorough job of closing the path to mature genitality for many of their sons and daughters, and an equally good job of leaving little cleared detours that led downhill to homosexual and infantile green pastures, and on to alcoholism, neuroses, divorce, to race-hate and brutality, and to a tight inflexible mind that could not question itself.

They did a thorough job of dishonoring love, of making honesty seem a treasonable thing, of leaving in their children an unquenchable need to feel superior to others, to bow easily to authority, and to value power and money more dearly than human relations and truth.

They did a thorough job of splitting the soul in two. They separated ideals from acts, beliefs from knowledge, and turned their children sometimes into exploiters but more often into moral weaklings who daydream about democracy and human dignity and freedom and integrity, yet cannot find the real desire to bring these dreams into reality; always they keep dreaming and hoping, and fearing, that the next generation will do it.

Sometimes I have grown tired of hearing Mom blamed for all that is wrong with her sons and daughters. After all, we might well ask, who started the grim mess? Who long ago made Mom and her sex "inferior" and stripped her of her economic and political and sexual rights? Who, nearly two thousand years ago, said, "It is good for a man not to touch a woman. . . . But if they cannot contain, let them marry: for it is better to marry than to burn"? Certainly that old misogynist St. Paul was no female apostle. Man, born of woman, has found it a hard thing to forgive her for giving him birth. The patriarchal protest against the ancient matriarch has borne strange fruit through the years. . . .

In speaking of millions of people and their customs, their feelings and values, we have to remind ourselves that many have not shared in experiences that have yet profoundly affected their whole lives. They have, instead, made identification with them. Experiences which others have had link themselves too easily sometimes with our secret fantasies and secret needs until a curious bond is woven of the actual experiences of the few and the unconscious desire of the many to possess them. A generation, free of wounds, will identify itself with the battle scars of a past generation in a masochistic community of daydreams because it needs to feel pain. Hanns Sachs has brilliantly reminded us in *The Creative Unconscious* of man's capacity to daydream in company with others when each has within him a secret fantasy that can be acted out in rhythm with others. Here in the artist is the seed of a dream growing into a book, a painting, a poem, which awakens deep down in the one beholding it another shadowy dream that, like a reflection in a pool, takes on mysterious shape and substance; and suddenly there is a profound communion of dream with dream, not on the bright surface of life but in the secret shadowy places of the spirit. It may be for only a moment in time, or for all of a life, but two fantasies have met, magically bridging time and space, and whispered their secrets to each other. This is art's power over us; and art's terror, for there are dreams we do not want aroused again, ash that must remain ash. And sometimes in blinding anger and fear we turn and rend a poem, a book, a painting, a truth that has blown too steadily on old forgotten graves of memories calling forth ghosts whom we have forbidden to walk the earth again. This is the secret of art. And of a people's myth also. This is the secret of tradition's hypnotic power over the minds of a whole region though most of those minds may know tradition only by hearsay.

Southern tradition, segregation, states' rights have soaked up the secret fears of our people; little private fantasies of childhood have crept there for hiding, unacknowledged arsenals of hate have been stored there, and a loyalty covering up a lack of mature love has glazed the words over with sanctity. No wonder the saying of them aloud can stir anxieties until there are times when it seems that we have lost our grasp of reality.

~ Part Three ~

Giants in the Earth

～ 1 ～

Distance and Darkness

ONLY A MAN or woman who has traveled in childhood the old sand or clay roads of the South in buggy or wagon, who has stayed in the country after nightfall, can know what distance and darkness meant in the making of the rural mind of the South.

Distance was not a word but an invisible force pushing a man hard against his memories and fears, isolating him by impenetrable walls from a world to which he had never felt securely tied. When the sun set, the night began. There were no lights; only a kerosene lamp, or lantern, a pine knot burning. And always the swamp back of you or the dark hills, or empty fields stretching on, on. . . . Far off, the Negroes singing in little dim lantern-lit churches, moaning their misery and shouting their joy. Sudden sharp laughter from nowhere.

City people, townspeople, have little idea what this meant, and still means in parts of the lonely South. During the war they felt the wear on nerves of the blackout, but country folks have lived in a blackout since time began. Darkness comes. Sounds creep out so stealthily: whippoorwill, tree-frogs, roar of alligator back in the pond, rustle of palmetto, restless, never-ending, as if an unseen hand brushes over it and cannot let go . . . the scream of a cat in the swamp. Sounds like these weave in and out of lonely fantasies, pulling in hearsay tales, making a tight mat of ideas and feelings and fancies and fears until one no longer knows the real from the unreal, and sometimes one no longer cares. The sweet things too: jessamine crawling on fences and trees, giving out a wonder of yellow fragrance, bays blooming white and delicate down in the swamp, and water lilies fattening on green pond water, making you love the loneliness you hate, making you want to stay even as you feel you must leave or die.

Sometimes as you sat there, crazy Miss Sue would walk down the road giggling to herself. You'd say, "Howdy, Miss Sue," and she would hurry past breathlessly as if to keep a late appointment or maybe she would stop, turn, look at you gently as if you were a childhood dream and then float away in the dusk. And you would watch her, bemused, not certain after a moment whether it was Miss Sue or your own strange notions walking down the road beyond you.

Sometimes a man sat on the front steps, talking a little about the crop or the next day's farm work, whittling on a stick, maybe just thinking, now and then aiming his spittle carefully to hit the bull's-eye of a totally imaginary spot. Have you seen that? That is rural adventure, rural fun! No wonder a man hunt took on zest, with no more thought given the running, frightened human being than to a running, frightened animal. One centered on one's own excitement. After all, the "best" people of the South, the leaders, the preachers, the writers, the editors, those who give value to living, said Negroes were less than human and were not to be treated as human while alive, why then did they have to die like humans! Out in the country, animals do not seem so different from men. Sometimes they seem closer to you than human beings, close enough that you want to mate with them, especially when you are young, and sometimes you do. But animals are killed to be eaten, or when they get in the way. . . . Blood-letting is a thing one gets used to in the country. Hog-killing . . . sticking a pig, hanging it up, listening to those human-like squeals, watching blood streak the flesh. . . . Negro-killing. . . . So strangely akin—in sick minds that hold no words to stop the hand.

Southern culture has put few words in the mind to make the difference between human and animal. The words in the white mind are words that turn the Negro into animal, words deliberately fed to people to place the Negro beneath the level of human, to make him not only animal but a "menace." So much cruelty is on almost a somatic level. It is a man's dreams that make him human or inhuman and a man who knows few words to dream with, who has never heard, in words said aloud, other men's dreams of human dignity and freedom and tender love, and brotherhood, who has never heard of man the creator of truth and beauty, who has never even seen man-made beauty, but has heard only of man the killer, and words about sex and "race" which fill him with anger and fear and lust, and words about himself that make him feel degraded, or blow him up crazily into paranoid "superiority"—how can he know the meaning of *human!* How can he know that? Only his own mother's love for him and his love for her, and his love for his own child, have given him a conception of human love; that is all he knows of tenderness; and there have been few words in his mind to help him transfer this tenderness to other human beings, few symbols out of which to create bridges between himself and the rest of the earth's people.

Sometimes, when even his mother had not given him love, and tenderness had been withheld from him and too much guilt laid on him, and loneliness had lasted too long and darkness had forced his eyes to turn inward on sights he could not bear to remember, then something got into a man. A man hunt then became not an animal-killing or a fox hunt but a break-through of perverse sex feelings and deep bitter hatred known in childhood; and when this happened, no cruelty seemed enough to satisfy the hunger that drove men on. Such a man hunt is a journey into all that has been forbidden by religion and by women, a group flight into a strange free land of fury which the rational mind finds hard to understand. It is like the violent murders we read about in the newspapers or have known to happen on our own street: the good man, superintendent of Sunday school who, one morning at breakfast, turns and shoots down his children, his wife, then himself. Or the girl, sweet, demure, gentle, who walks in one evening and kills her mother, hacking her body to pieces in a terrible fury that has devoured—like cancer devours the healthy body cells—all the sane love-tissue of her spirit. At such times of fury a mere killing is not enough. One is not satisfied that "the enemy" be dead; one must tear up and mutilate so that there is nothing left to remind one that a person once existed. It is as if one must destroy the very memory of a relationship, tearing every fiber of it out of one's life as the body is torn to pieces.

Only a few of our people are killers; only a handful would take a man's life so greedily. But there have been too many lynchings in the South of this nature where the Negro—a stranger to the mob who lynched him—has not only been shot but his body riddled with bullets (each person in the group killing the lifeless body again and again and again), for us not to understand that the lynched Negro becomes *not an object that must die* but a receptacle for every man's dammed-up hate, and a receptacle for every man's forbidden sex feelings. Sex and hate, cohabiting in the darkness of minds too long, pour out their progeny of cruelty on anything that can serve as a symbol of an unnamed relationship that in his heart each man wants to kill and befoul. That, sometimes, the lynchers do cut off genitals of the lynched and divide them into bits to be distributed to participants as souvenirs is no more than a coda to this composition of hate and guilt and sex hunger and fear, created by our way of life in the South, and by our families and by our ideas of right and wrong.

No wonder lynchings—even one or two a year—shock us deeply, for each one is a Sign, not so much of troubled race relations, as of a troubled way of life that threatens to rise up and destroy all the people who live it. And just as one lynching in Dixie shakes the whole world, poised as it is today in such delicate equilibrium, so do the efforts to make lynching a national crime upset on deep unverbalized levels of the mind those southern leaders and their northern associates who gave the privilege of lynching to rural whites as a ritualistic reward for accepting so meekly their design for living, who protected it through the years, and who now dread the withdrawal of this compensation, knowing well that the design will crumble quickly, and not knowing at all what will follow thereafter, either in their region or in their own minds.

But it is not only the few murderers, and the few political leaders, who are guilty. It is ourselves. Without our silent permission this violence of word and deed could never be.

Distance and darkness have set the rural South apart from the rest of our nation. Darkness of mind and of countryside. And terrifying ignorance. What good does it do to repeat illiteracy figures to readers whose minds have been nourished well since they were born? How can we who were fed so bountifully feel what it means to live with a mind emptied of words, bereft of ideas and facts, unknowing of books and man-made beauty, any more than our well-fed bodies can feel the weakness of a body that has never had a full meal but has survived somehow on a starvation diet! To know that the South's average literacy is fifth grade, that until the New Deal almost no rural counties had libraries, that few Georgia rural families even now read any newspaper except the county paper, the *Statesman*, or the Augusta *Courier*, is not to understand, but sometimes only to shield one's mind with facts from feeling such mental emptiness.

Distance and darkness and starvation, and ignorance, and malaria and heat ate like vultures on our rural people, not for a few war years but for two centuries.

But worse things happened. We cannot forget that these rural people *were not let alone*. It would have been far better for them had they been ignored, as have been most of the peasants of the world until communism's recent efforts, as, in so many ways, the southern poor whites were let alone during the days of slavery, and as the mountain whites were largely ignored until the past three or four decades. But the southerners in the dominant group—as Russians today need peasants—needed the so-called "poor whites" after the Civil War and used them as ruthlessly as Negroes were used when they were needed. They needed their bodies to work for them when industries came South; they needed their votes in a democracy, and in a democracy there are ways to get votes; they needed, with a curious urgency—for democracy makes you want your fellow men to like you—the poor whites' mass approval of acts that the dominant group's more informed, educated minds, ambivalent hearts, and Christian-trained souls could never wholly approve. They needed poor whites to be their yes-men, moral henchmen quieting their leaders' uneasy consciences. Like David playing on his harp to Saul, the rural whites sang the lies the dominant group wanted to hear, but they were lies that not David but Saul had composed, though Saul never more than half believed them. It was only the poor-white Davids who learned to love these lies which they needed sorely to believe were true. To be "superior," to be the "best people on earth" with the best "system" of making a living, because your sallow skin was white and you were "Anglo-Saxon," made you forget that you were eaten up with malaria and hookworm; made you forget that you lived in a shanty and ate pot-likker and corn bread, and worked long hours for nothing. Nobody could take away from you this whiteness that made you and your way of life "superior." They could take your house, your job, your fun; they could steal your wages, keep you from acquiring knowledge; they could tax your vote or cheat you out of it; they could by arousing your anxieties make you sexually impotent; but they could not strip your white skin off of you. It became the poor white's most precious possession, a symbol of self-esteem and psychic security, a "charm" staving off utter dissolution. And in devious, perverse ways it helped maintain his sanity in an insane world, compensating him—as did his church's promise of heaven—for so many spiritual bruises and material deprivations. For though their religion took most of the rural whites' pleasures away from them, dirtying sex and the human body until it was a nasty thing, making dancing and card playing and the drinking of even a glass of beer wrong, thus adding severe strains to bodies already drained by poverty and ill health and loneli-ness, yet the revivalists did give them reassuring promise of

food, raiment, and golden pleasures in heaven, telling them
again and again that Jesus died so their souls could be saved
after death, from hell; and though they did nothing about
starved minds and bodies, nothing about health and jobs,
demagogues did keep their starved spirits alive here on
earth with the drug of white supremacy and Negro-hate
which the revivalists never named as "sins." Listening to
words of revivalist and demagogue, the poor white, despite
his misery, believed himself important among men for Jesus
had died for him, and his "white blood" made him superior
to all other people: "niggers," "furriners," Jews. All you had
to do was to "believe" in Jesus and to hate all unbelievers,
to be "saved" in heaven; and to "believe" in white supremacy
and to hate and shun all who were different, to be "set apart"
here on earth as supreme. "Oh, wash me, and I shall be
whiter than snow, whiter than snow, yes, whiter than snow,"
was to white Christian supremacy: a song crooned by millions to lull themselves into one vast communal daydream, in
order to escape a too-hard reality.

It is impossible to understand these pitiful delusions of
grandeur, clung to so tenaciously by millions of impoverished, ignorant, lonely, confused people unless one is willing
to look for not "one cause" but a series of causes and effects
spiralling back through the centuries.

These people were the rejected of Europe, and feeling
their rejection, they rebelled against those forces that had
injured them. They were hurt people, "agin the world" that
had hurt them; refugees, seeking escape from too-heavy
pressures, who came to a warm humid climate where new
pressures, new enemies awaited them: malaria, typhoid, wild
animals, Indians, loneliness, and a new cultural conflict
whose seeds had begun to sprout in 1619 when the first

African was taken off a Dutch man-of-war in Virginia. Many
of the refugees had lived in the slums of European and
English cities and knew little of the land and how to make
a good living from it. Others (in later decades) fled the
potato famine in Ireland, and were embittered and frightened by unseen enemies who had almost proved their un-
doing. They came to the new country as if to a promised
land, eager to "begin again"; not to change themselves, not
to understand their past experiences, but simply to "begin
again" with the same old selves in a new setting; and a few
came to the new country in blind psychic flight moving in
the direction which the fresh strong wind of a new age
opened up most easily to them.

Most of them had never read a printed page. Few, even
of their leaders, were men who possessed educated minds.
They had never learned to look at the past or understand it
as it had been experienced either by them or by their ancestors. Actually, there were few pages of the past clear
enough for the most learned to read. Science was only beginning to roll back the fog that covered the universe. Names
like Galileo and Copernicus and Descartes had never been
heard by most of these early settlers; Newton had not been
born when the first slave was landed in Virginia; the theory
of evolution was not a controversy, it was hardly a dream
when many of the religious refugees fled English shores. But
there was a feeling which most men felt—nurtured through
centuries by the Catholic Church which profited so highly
from ignorance and later by the Protestant Church also—
that knowledge was "wrong" and only faith was "right." The
darkness was good because men had always stumbled
around in it; ignorance was natural because men had been
bruised on it so long; one's belief is more important than
what *is,* for one has never known what *is;* one's fantasy is

more "real" than reality; the familiar, though it destroy you, is better than the strange, though it heal you. And believing this, they feared the lighting of one small candle of knowledge that might push back the darkness and show what was really there. No wonder they turned away and shrieked in fear and anger when science began to swing great searchlights across the universe, and to send up hypotheses like flares into the unknown!

And though the new winds of science and discovery also blew fine shining words across the world, of man's importance, of human "rights," that fell on men's minds like an accolade, singling them out one by one, individual by individual, from the anonymous mass, making them blink with the sudden honor awarded them as persons, most of these settlers in the New World reached out only for those words they liked, and of these, *I am as good as you* were the words their wounded spirits needed and they rubbed them like salve on their lacerated egos, forgetting often in their self-concern to share the salve with others.

This profound fear of scientific knowledge, this leaning on an Authority for a faith to believe in, the rebellious refugees brought with them to America from a Europe still medieval in thought. And as they moved southward along the Appalachian trails into the mountain coves and valleys, farther and farther from the knowledge, the new science, that Europe was just beginning to hear about, or followed the rivers from the southern coast into the rich lands where they built their great farms or their new towns or their lonely little shacks in lonely woods and fields, they clung to this feeling as if to a part of their body, ready to attach it like an umbilical cord to the Authority which offered them the most ease in the new land. For all a rebel ever does (until he matures enough to hold his own intelligence as his final authority) is to exchange one authority for another, reaching for the new, even as he rejects the old, or returning to the old after becoming disillusioned by the new. Unable to nourish himself with food which has been masticated in his own mind he depends upon others for nourishment, as does the infant on a "formula" food presented him in a nippled bottle.

Once in the new country, once settled along river or edge of swamp or in lonely stretches of black rich soil, the refugees were cut off from the Europe they both hated and secretly loved, and the clock of European culture stopped ticking for them, its hands fixed on the edge of medieval times.

The winds of science sweeping across the cities of Europe and America, bending men's ideas and ways, uprooting them, re-arranging them in three centuries as they had not been changed in ten thousand years, were not felt by these isolated men and women who could not read or write, who sometimes in a lifetime did not meet one traveler from Europe or from the city centers of culture in America, who heard only the traveling preachers and later the traveling politicians who were as isolated and ignorant as they.

Cut off now from the old, each refugee began to live his life, weaving it of his inner needs and conflicts and dreams and of the new external circumstances as he found them. Those whose energies were free, who could work, who valued money and material possessions, got them by reaching out and exploiting circumstances, accidents, and people to their advantage.

The black man fell into their design and was made the most of. Land was acquired, money saved, more land and slaves purchased, homes built, possessions accumulated, and new powers felt. By the time of the Civil War in 1861, only one-tenth of one per cent of these old refugee families owned as many slaves as did Scarlett O'Hara's family; only two and one-half per cent owned four or more slaves. But 200,000 families out of 5,600,000 whites did own at least one slave and the ownership of one human being as slave is enough to put a Christian's conscience and mind in bondage for a lifetime. For though one slave profits him little yet always he hopes for heavier profits since he has invested so much of his integrity in the system which now he is compelled to defend. And, though eighty per cent did not own even one slave and continued their small living from tilling the soil, or from hunting and trapping or the setting up of shops where the services needed by rural people could be met, many hoped some day to own one and thought of themselves as slave-holding people, identifying in fantasy with the plantation South, especially after their defeat in the Civil War—as the popularity of *Gone With the Wind*, not only among those whose families were once planters but among the very poor, demonstrated.

The talent for identifying with the more fortunate Jones —the word *class* suggests a rigidity that even in the gentleman-conscious South never existed—is as American as Daniel Boone and corn bread. By hooking on in fantasy to those who possess more, who have achieved more, who have "succeeded," we spin a ladder out of hope and self-confidence and dreams which we Americans blithely climb though it swing dizzily through endless space. Some fall but so many succeed in climbing from mud to stars that all believe in their hearts that it can be done. No wealth, no learning, no fame, no office, no achievement, and no goodness seems beyond the grasp of the most poor and ignorant and lowdown white American. And this is still true, even though depressions have battered great numbers of our people back

into the mud, geographical frontiers have disappeared, and
certain rigidities in industrial cities have set in. It may have
been a kind of euphoria that fixed itself on the refugees who,
bruised and insecure, found themselves in a vast open
country of limitless resources; it was certainly due in part
to the *I am as good as you* that democracy came to mean to
most of them; it undoubtedly was strengthened by the white-
skin-color fetish which they wore in their minds like a rab-
bit's foot, but this talent for identifying came also from the
simple fact that so many of the very poor and ignorant were
kin to the very rich or learned, and nearly all were kin to
those scattered on various levels between the aristocratic
planter and the "mud sill."

All of them, rich and poor, lived for a long time off the
soil, which they gouged out as ruthlessly as the pugnacious
among them gouged each other's eyes out. (One of the first
laws put on statute books in Georgia forbade the gouging
out of a man's eyes.) Only a people aggressive, wasteful, and
greedy could have stripped the soil, and the forest, of richness as did these southern settlers. Raping, tearing it, taking
what they needed from it, then throwing it aside, uncaring
what happened to it, was an outward expression, an acting
out, too often, of their secret feelings about women and sex.
The gullied land of the South, washed-out and eroded,
matched the washed-out women of the rural South whose
bodies were too often used as ruthlessly as was the land;
who worked hard as the animals; who submitted to a sexual
intercourse sometimes rough, coarse, furtive (unknowing
that love-making can be gay and tender, though in recent
decades some, learning to read romances and attending the
movies, secretly believe it in their fantasies); who bore children in great pain because their culture (and sometimes
their church) was uncaring that they, as human beings,

suffered; who were often segregated in church (as were the Negroes in old days), sitting on separate pews from the men; who were not thought fit to be citizens and to vote until three decades ago; and who in some states cannot own property except in their husband's name; who, even now, cannot officiate as ministers in most of the churches though they keep the breath of life in the church. No wonder a demagogue talking on rural courthouse steps can buy the votes of these malnourished, worn-out, lonely women of the South, with his talk of "sacred womanhood" and "purity" and "protecting our women from the menace of Negroes," for he is buying votes with a dream.

In the early spring of 1948, one of Mississippi's politicians delivered himself of this tribute which reaches a high peak even for southern chivalry:

Now what of the ladies? When God made the Southern woman he summoned His angel messengers and He commanded them to go through all the star-strewn vicissitudes of space and gather all there was of beauty, of brightness and sweetness, of enchantment and glamor, and when they returned and laid the golden harvest at His feet He began in their wondering presence the work of fashioning the Southern girl. He wrought with the golden gleam of the stars, with the changing colors of the rainbow's hues and the pallid silver of the moon. He wrought with the crimson that swooned in the rose's ruby heart, and the snow that gleams on the lily's petal; then, glancing down deep into His own bosom, He took of the love that gleamed there like pearls beneath the sun-kissed waves of a summer sea, and thrilling this love into the form He had fashioned, all heaven veiled its face, for lo, He had wrought the Southern girl. . . .

Listening, many weary, lonely country women who have never had a chance to be *persons,* who have rarely felt esteemed or tenderly beloved, are suddenly caught up by a vision of themselves as Sacred Womanhood on a Pedestal, as Southern Madonnas, and though in a few hours they will be back totin' slops to the pigpen, milking cows, cooking supper, yet for a moment, for one miraculously sweet breath of time, they are transfigured by this image of themselves and they will never forget the moment. A vote, which is drawing a few lines through names on a piece of paper, is a small thing to give a man who has made you feel cherished and beloved and revered for the first time in your life.

As time went on, generation breeding generation in warm humid climate, as circumstance piled high on circumstance to make a living easier for the few and harder for the many, large groups of rural southerners grew less inclined to "better themselves," and more effortless in their living. The old pioneer community of interests, the simple rural democracy of men sharing equally in danger and disease and duties was cracking apart. Those who were ambitious, greedy, healthy, and luckier continued to gather around them slaves and more slaves, and more and more land, pushing the others to the edge of the slave system and off the rich land, closer to swamps and hills. Sometimes a man became slave owner not only because of a good headstart given him by greed, physical energy, and ambition but by a small or large land grant in the old days from the Crown. It happened too in a family that one son loved money above all else and his brother seemed not to care for money at all. It happened more rarely that a man had a conscience about this matter of slavery while another accepted it easily as the "right" of the white race. Such separations as these came about in families until after a generation or so, wealthy planters had seedy-looking cousins back in the poor lands, and po' folks could claim to be "blood kin" to the richest folks in the county.

A thousand such accidents—health, temperament, glands, conscience, greed, and luck—like a giant hand pushed the few into great wealth and the many away from it. And though always there were those in between, owners of small farms or service shops, and the doctors, lawyers, preachers of the region, a separation began in minds that had already taken place in living: a chasm between rich and poor that washed deeper and deeper as the sweat of more and more slaves poured in it. Those on the other side of the chasm from the large slave owner—and that was most of the South —came to be called "poor whites" and "crackers," "red necks," "hill billies," and "peckerwoods," and a startling lack of sympathy for them slipped into speech and writings and hearts of the planter class.

When one looks today at our southern people and their land and their homes it becomes so obvious that our way of life—our white-supremacy and sharecropping system, our values—has never worked. Perhaps part of the hatred felt by the successful ones seeps out of this bitter fact. The few who have profited down through the years know that they, or their fathers, have fattened off the misery and ignorance and fears and tensions of the majority of our people and they are made uncomfortable by this knowledge. They feel that if they can only shut themselves away from Tobacco Road by closing eyes, maybe then Tobacco Road will no longer exist. And yet, in the rural South we live too close to each other ever to shut the sight away. It rolls into our back yards, into our filling stations, into our stores and doctors' offices on Saturdays. The only way to escape such misery is to shut one's mind against it.

And the successful ones of the South have done so. They have not only shut out the bad, they have shut out the good. They deny Tobacco Road, rub it off of the maps of their region, and yet too often they secretly think of the rural white as a Tobacco Roader. They discredit him because he is poor and without learning. They snub him, make jokes about him sometimes in their newspapers. They fear him as if every rural white is a potential lyncher or Klansman, yet only a small number of our people have taken part in physical violence. They have written him off as a liability to democracy, expecting him to vote for demagogues, expecting him to be against human rights for all men, against all that is good and creative. The dominant group in the South fear him because they know they have kept from him not only jobs and living wages and hospitals and housing and recreation, but they have kept from him also the dream of the free responsible human being. Knowing this, in their fear and guilt, they cannot acknowledge the good that is still in our people.

And yet, in spite of poverty, sickness, loneliness, ignorance, the majority of our southern rural people have qualities that are genuine assets to our nation: a kindness in personal relationships, a sense of humor, a sturdy belief in their own worth, a courtesy in community relations, a stoicism that bends rather than breaks under strain, and a wistful desire "to be good."

This conscience of our rural people is a potent force for good. In spite of the church's strange and terrible evasion of those beliefs concerning human worth and brotherhood and love that Jesus preached, in spite of its cruel emphasis on punishment and guilt, it has taught our rural people to love this Galilean who lived so close to the poor. His name they treat with reverence. There is no political figure on earth that can compete with him in their hearts. Image after image that is tender and compassionate floats through their memory from childhood, gentling their lives. The Child and its Mother, the Christmas story, the Sermon on the Mount, these are real experiences that are woven through the texture of their minds. They may fear God and hell but they love and believe in Jesus. And if his teachings were translated into contemporary terms they would follow them. The desire is there. They want to "do right." It is a tragic thing that this "right" has been so distorted and cheapened that we can recognize in it so few of the words that Jesus spoke.

I live in the country and know my neighbors well. I have watched the families around me as they have reared their children. A few live in unpainted houses on wages that in the depression were sometimes no more than $40.00 per month for a family of eight. Sometimes they have not had much to eat but in most of the families I know the children have had an abundant diet of love and good will. They are accepted children. The training is less compulsive than one often finds among the "privileged" families. In spite of all they have heard at church, bodies are usually accepted as the natural habitat for the human spirit; parental ambitions do not harden like a millstone around young shoulders. Sunshine helps too, and open fields to run in, and working with the farm animals, and sharing the family responsibilities one with another. Whatever the reasons for it, rural parents—in spite of poverty and isolation—have sometimes done a better job of child-rearing than have the wealthy in towns and cities. There are always those who fail, who because of ignorance and their own frustrations cripple their children's characters, but there are too many who are good parents for us to underestimate the magnificent possibilities for a rich creative life that our people hold within them.

It is the community that has failed the rural child by failing to provide adequate schools and health clinics, hospital care, libraries, art centers, and facilities for group recreation, jobs for their fathers, and housing to take the place of the southern shacks that stereotype our landscape.

And it has failed also by providing almost no leadership that has communicated to child and parent those beliefs which increase the stature of men as human beings but has left this, the most important job in a democracy, to demagogues.

As we look across the world, we see the rural people not only of our own country but of China and India, Burma, Europe, Africa turning like giants in the earth, with their new powers. And we know as we watch that the beliefs they hold will make or destroy our own future. It is not a good thing to remember how little we have done to communicate to them by act or word the dream of human dignity and freedom that we believe in.

~ 2 ~

Two Men and a Bargain

ONCE UPON a time, down South, Mr. Rich White made a bargain with Mr. Poor White. He studied about it a long time before he made it, for it had to be a bargain Mr. Poor White would want to keep forever. It's not easy to make a bargain another man will want to keep forever, and Mr. Rich White knew this. So he looked around for something to put in it that Mr. Poor White would never want to take out.

He looked around . . . and his eyes fell on the Negro. I've got it, he whispered.

He called in Mr. Poor White and said, "I've been thinking a lot about you and me lately—how hard it is for us to make a living down here with no money and the rest of the country against us. To keep my farm and mill going the way I want them to go, making big profit off of little capital, I have to keep wages low, you can see that. It's the only way I can make as much as I want to make as quickly as I want to make it. And folks coming in from the North have to keep wages low too, for that's our southern tradition.

174

"It's a good way for us rich folks and it's not bad for you either, for you're smart enough to see that any job's better than no job at all. And you know too that whatever's wrong with the South isn't my fault or your fault but is bound to be the Yankee's fault or the fault of those freight rates. . . .

"For instance, the nigger. You don't need *me* to tell you that ever since the damyankee freed him, the nigger's been scrouging you, pushing you off your land, out of your job, jostling you on the sidewalks, all time biggity. If he hadn't been freed, he'd never bothered you, for I could have kept him on the farm and bossed him like I bossed him for 200 years. But the damyankees always know better, don't they! Here I am busy at my mill with no time to boss him, and here he is in your way, scrouging you, causing lot of trouble. Thing I can't forget is your skin's the color of my skin and we're both made in God's image; we're white men and white men can't let a nigger scrouge 'em.

"There're two big jobs down here that need doing: Somebody's got to tend to the living, and somebody's got to tend to the nigger. Now, I've learned a few things about making a living you're too no-count to learn (else you'd be making money same way I make it): things about jobs and credit, prices, hours, wages, votes, and so on. But one thing you can learn easy, any white man can, is how to handle the black man. Suppose now you take over the thing you can do and let me take over the thing I can do. What I mean is, you boss the nigger, and I'll boss the money. How about it?

"Anything you want to do to show folks you're boss you're free to do it. You can run the schools and the churches any way you want to. You can make the customs and set the manners and write the laws (long as you don't touch my business). You can throw books out of libraries if you don't like what's in them and you can decide pretty much what kind of learning, if any, you want southern children to have. If science scares you and you don't like the notion of messing around with it, remember you don't have to, this is God's country and a free one. Anyway, it'll tell you things you can't believe and still believe what you believe now so it's better maybe not to take much stock in it.

"If you ever get restless when you don't have a job or your roof leaks, or the children look puny and shoulder blades stick out more than natural, all you need do is remember you're a sight better off and better than the black man. And remember this too: There's nothing so good for folks as to go to church on Sundays. To show you I believe this, I'll build you all the churches down at the mill and on the farm you want—just say the word.

"But if you get nervous sometimes anyway, and don't have much to do, and begin to get worried-up inside and mad with folks, and you think it'll make you feel a little better to lynch a nigger occasionally, that's OK by me too; and I'll fix it with the sheriff and the judge and the court and our newspapers so you won't have any trouble afterwards; but *don't expect me to come to the lynching, for I won't be there.*

"Now, if folks are fool enough to forget they're white men, if they forget that, I'm willing to put out plenty money to keep the politicians talking, and I don't mind supporting a real first-class demagogue or two, to say what you want him to say—just so he does what I want about my business. And I promise you this: Long as you keep the Negro out of your unions, we'll keep him out of our mills. We'll give you the pick of what jobs there are, and if things get too tight you can take over his jobs also, for any job's better than no job at all. Now that's a bargain. Except, of course, if you're ever crazy enough to strike or stir up labor legislation, or let the niggers into your unions, or mess around with the vote, then we'll have to use the black folks, every goddam one of them maybe, to teach you a lesson. We'll tell folks—or our politicians will—that you're mongrelizing the white race with your unions, we'll tell 'em you're so lowdown you're begging the nigger to be your social equal, and if that won't work, we'll tell them the black man is after your women. We have ways and we'll use them.

"Best thing you can do, seems to me, is to Jim Crow everything. It'll be easier for us that way to keep the niggers out of the unions and down on the farm where they belong, and it ought to make you feel better for a lot of reasons. For one thing, you can ride with us in the front of the streetcar and bus and shove the colored folks plumb onto the back seat. You'll like that and we won't mind much either—though God knows you can stink as bad as any of 'em when you go round dirty. But we'll put up with it, for we don't ride the streetcars and buses much anyway, and we can see how it makes you feel a lot better to know you can sit up with us and the black man can't sit there; even if he's a college professor, he can't sit there, remember! So fix that up any way you say. And you can do the same about trains and waiting rooms and toilets and movies and schools and churches and so on. And you can make rules about restaurants and hotels too if it'll make you feel better. And I reckon it will, though you aren't likely ever to go into one of the hotels or restaurants you put your Jim Crow rule on. But even if you don't have money to go inside one of them, it'll make you feel good to know you're sort of bossing things there. . . . So go on and fix all the Jim Crow you want. When you don't have meat to eat and milk for the younguns, you can eat Jim Crow and if you don't think too much about it, you'll never know the difference, for you don't seem to have much sense, anyway."

And Mr. Rich White and Mr. Poor White thought they'd made a good bargain.

It never occurred to Mr. Rich White that with a bargain the Negro could help him make money. It never occurred to Mr. Poor White that with a bargain the Negro could help him raise wages. For neither ever thought about the Negro as somebody who could help folks make money. Neither ever thought about him as somebody who could make a real bargain. Always the Negro was somebody who took things away, scraps and taxes, prestige, shoddy and second-hand things, but things away from you. Always he was something you had to prove you were better than, and you couldn't prove it, no you couldn't prove it. And always he was something you had to hate and be afraid of. It was sometimes like this: If he wasn't human like you said, if he wasn't, you'd never know what he might do, you couldn't count on him; he might do all the things you had wanted to do or dreamed about doing that you knew were not human, all the kinds of things you know other folks would want to do if they were not human. And sometimes it was like this: If you once let yourself believe he is human, then you'd have to admit you'd done things to him you can't admit you've done to a human. You'd have to know you'd done things that God would send you to hell for doing. . . . And sometimes it was like this: You just hated him. Hated and feared and dreaded him, for you could never forget, there was no way to forget, what you'd done to his women and to those women's children; there was no way of forgetting your dreams of those women. . . . No way of forgetting. . . .

Yes . . . they thought they had a good bargain.

They felt pretty easy about things for a while, for it seemed that this would fix anything. They proudly told the world that the South had no Negro problem, it was all settled. They bragged that nobody understood the Negro like the South did, nobody understood the South's business like the South did, nobody understood southern labor like the South did, and the South had fixed things up. Yes, had fixed things up all right for Mr. Rich White and Mr. Poor White and the Negro.

(And Mr. Rich White from the North came South and saw how it worked and went home and told folks about it. Those southerners may be touchy, he said, but they know how to fix things. There's nothing that would help us more up North than to fix things up the way they've fixed them. With the Negroes coming up now in droves, we can do it, if we bring Jim Crow up with them. Thing for us to do is get restrictive covenants started and segregate without putting up signs. Folks up North might be embarrassed over the signs. But if you're smart, you can segregate without signs, and if you get it going, Jews and a lot of other folks can be segregated along with the Negroes. They have a lot of slogans we can use up here too, things like *you can't legislate hate,* and *change comes slowly,* and don't forget the one about your sister. It'll work in the North as well as in the South. As a matter of fact the Republicans would do well to keep the bargain with the Dixie politicians they made in 1876. That's the best way to stop communistic liberals! And the North listened, and it wasn't long before they too began to fix things. . . .)

Down South, folks began keeping their bargain. They began keeping their bargain to segregate southern living. They segregated southern money from Mr. Poor White and they segregated southern mores from Mr. Rich White and they segregated southern churches from Christianity, and they segregated southern minds from honest thinking, and they segregated the Negro from everything. And it wasn't long before everybody knew about Jim Crow and talked about Jim Crow and thought about Jim Crow and Jim Crow took on a great importance.

Jim Crow was Mr. Rich White's idea but Mr. Poor White made it work. Mr. Poor White put his mind on it and his time, for he had plenty of time when he didn't have a job, and he made it work. He had ways. Lynching was a good way, and so was flogging. Burning folks' houses was another way. And all these ways eased the feeling he had that he'd lost something, made him almost believe he had found it. . . . And sometimes it eased things in Mr. Rich White's heart also.

But again and again Mr. Rich White's sons and daughters, or his kinfolks or his friends' children who worked for him, or the poor white's children who somehow or other got to college and into good jobs, would forget that Jim Crow is important; and others among them whose hearts refused to go along with southern custom, would try not to practice it; and sometimes a newspaper man who wrote for the rich man would write a brave editorial; and sometimes a preacher who was supported by the rich man would preach about Jesus and love and brotherhood. But not for long. No, not for long. For Mr. Poor White would show them. Mr. Poor White would remind Mr. Rich White of their bargain. Sometimes he did it by coming to the office and talking. But most times he did it more simply by going out and lynching a Negro, or burning a house down, or burning crosses before other folks' houses, or starting a riot, or smearing nasty lies on a man's name until he was sickened to silence. . . .

And Mr. Rich White, seeing these things, would remember. He would remember that Jim Crow is important to everybody. And he'd tell his newspaper man and his preacher and his teacher and his children and the poor white's children who worked for him and all the others that they must remember not to talk about human dignity and love and brotherhood, for talk like that stirs up trouble. They must remember the bargain and hush . . . hush their talking, hush their mind from its questions, hush their hearts from feeling human.

If Mr. Poor White broke the bargain, if he talked too much about unions or tried to organize new unions where there hadn't been unions, or tried to get Negroes into unions, then the other poor whites fixed him. Most times it was Mr. Rich White's idea; sometimes the poor whites'; but they fixed him. They flogged him, or feathered and tarred him, or ran him out of town, or shot him down like you would a hound dog. And they knew they could do it and nothing would happen. They knew they were free to lynch and flog, to burn and threaten each other and nothing would happen, for they had a bargain. They had a bargain with Mr. Rich White and he'd fix the police and the papers and the court and the judge and the jury and the preacher so nothing would happen.

Mr. Poor White felt his power and he used it. He raised hell with Negroes on buses and streetcars and day coaches whenever he felt the need to raise hell. He threw books out of libraries and tore up magazines whenever he didn't like what was in them. And sometimes just because he could not read or write, he had fun tearing them up. He decided when something could or couldn't be taught, whenever he wanted to. He decided on folks' morals: when they could drink liquor and when they couldn't, how they must treat their wives, what they could say about sex and God and science and country and the Negro—and how they could say it; and the manners they could use toward other people. He said when you could and when you couldn't use the word *mister;* when you could and when you couldn't tip your hat to a lady; who could come in your front door and who must go to your back door; who your friends could be and who your friends couldn't be. He told the newspapers what they could say and how they could say it—except about money. (Mr. Rich White told them about money.) He told the preachers what they could preach and how they must preach it—except about money. (Mr. Rich White told them about money.) He told the teachers what they could teach and how they must teach it—except about money. He was boss and he knew it. Boss of the Negro and boss of the white, boss of your home though you might never invite him in it; boss of your church though he might not worship with you; boss of everything in Dixie but the money. Boss of everything but Mr. Rich White's way of making money. Boss of everything but wages and hours and prices and jobs and credit and the vote, and his own living.

Sometimes the newspaper man or the preacher or the professor or the social worker, or a writer, sometimes a group of church women, or his own children, went to Mr. Rich White. "This thing can't go on," they'd say, for they were worried; worried and troubled and dismayed, though it was hard to find words for their feelings. Worried at the poor white's starving and diseased and towering stature; worried when they remembered colored friends, old playmates, and beloved childhood nurses; worried about that poor, frayed word *democracy* which a lot of them still believed in, and heartsick, for some would have liked to be decent and some cherished truth and freedom, and some still hungered to be loyal to the teachings of Jesus, and some knew simply that change must come to keep the earth from destruction and must come quickly.

Mostly they called their worry "the Negro problem," and sometimes it was "civil rights" or "the recent lynching" or "the flogging incident" or the Ku Klux Klan or "our school system" or "increasing crime" or "the health of the under-privileged" or "bad housing." And sometimes those more brave talked simply of human dignity and of hungry people, hungry and jobless and homeless and ignorant and bewildered black and white people. But few dared talk against segregation; few dared question the bargain.

All wanting Mr. Rich White to do something. All wanting things to be different, yet afraid to say aloud what they wanted.

Mr. Rich White would listen and smile to hide his own worry. Smile and say easy, if ladies were present, "You've let the Yankee papers upset you. You've let the Communists get you confused. Things we must remember, folks, is the poor white's feeling. No use to make him mad about little things. No use to do that, is there? You keep talking about calling Negroes 'mister,' using words like that in the papers, you'll make him mighty mad, won't you? You'll make him mad if you say so much about Negro schooling. You'll make him mad talking about equal salaries for colored and white teachers, and higher education. He won't like it. You'll make him mighty mad talking about the white primary for you know he'd rather not vote himself than have Negroes voting. You know that, don't you? You'll make him crazy mad talking about jobs for Negroes, jobs in the mills for colored folks. He doesn't want them working side by side with him. You'll hurt his morale talking about Jim Crow in the army, you can't do it! You got him upset now talking about science books and freedom of thinking. He don't want his children doubting God or thinking too much about anything. I'm not so sure myself but it's science and too much thinking that's wrong with all of us—the whole world, maybe, thinks too much about everything!

"And you can't write about lynchings and riots right after they've happened. Maybe when there hasn't been one in a long time, you should say a little something, something about lynching being a disgrace, bad as a principle, and about the Klan being uncivilized. But not right after there's been an incident in your own town. You'll only stir up trouble if you do it. You've got to keep things like that out of the papers. Thing we got to do, folks, is to keep *everything* out of the papers—except talk against the damyankee's meddling. Way to make things better is for everybody to hush talking."

And after the folks had left, Mr. Rich White would sit a while thinking; then he'd call in his newspaper boys and he'd tell 'em. "Better keep off of all those problems. Better write a piece about southern tradition. Better write a piece about segregation—that'll please the poor white and kind of calm him down—say it's here and nothing can change it, nothing can change it, nothing, not even Godamighty! Here wait— leave out that about God, just say *nothing can change it!* Better write something against union leaders, be easy on the workers but hard on their leaders. Say something about CIO being nigger-lover and Communist. That's always good. And something against Harlem Negroes and the NAACP and Walter White. Write something about Yankees meddling with our affairs and something against FEPC and the New Deal and make it plain that human rights are never as important as states' rights, but don't use *human*, think of some other way to say it. Keep saying that whatever is done about race has to be done by the South in its own way. Keep saying that. And be sure to say, 'Nobody but a fool would want to do away with segregation!' Better write plenty about unfair freight rates and the South being a colony of the North and about how wicked a place Harlem is. And wait a minute, boys—write something good about folks needing to read

their Bible and to go to church on Sunday, folks needing
the old-time religion."

Lord yes, Mr. Rich White whispered as he sat there thinking and worrying, got to make 'em know everybody had
better keep to his bargain, and everybody better get more
religion. A good old-fashioned revival would help us all
down here right now. Every one of us.

Sometimes the Negro would tap on Mr. Rich White's back
door, ease in, hat in hand, and say howdy. Sometimes he'd
tell Mr. Rich White what a fine man his father was and how
he is just like him. And then he'd ask a little favor. The favor
might be to borrow five dollars, or maybe it would seem just
as measly as that when the Negro said it, but it might be
about school books for the colored folks, or a new roof on the
church or the schoolhouse, or a raise for the teacher, or it
might even be about paving a street through Colored Town
or fixing a sewer line, or a playground, or a clinic for Negro
babies. But way the Negro said it, it'd sound nothing much,
and Mr. Rich White would think: It's the least I can do to
do it; and he'd say, "I don't see why we can't manage that,
Sam, glad you came in to see me." And the Negro would
leave, hat in hand, saying, "Thank you, Mr. Rich White,
thank you." And nobody would know but the Negro that
Mr. Rich White had broken his bargain with Mr. Poor White.
Nobody would catch on but the Negro. But the Negro knew.
He knew too from three centuries of learning that if you want
something from Mr. Rich White or his sons and his daughters
you ask it as a favor and not something due you, for Mr.
Rich White made his bargain with Mr. Poor White and the
white North made a bargain with the white South but nobody's made a bargain with the Negro.

That's right. Nobody made a bargain with the Negro. He

just kept on living without one. Kept gnawing the bones from Mr. Rich White's beefsteak, drinking the potlikker from Mr. Poor White's turnip greens, taking Mr. Rich White's favors, wearing his second-hand clothes, picking up the jobs Mr. Poor White threw him, riding the back seat, going in the back door, but going. . . .

And nobody thought anything due him, for the Negro never knew he had a bargain. All he did was keep going . . . singing, dancing, working, lying and stealing, fighting himself . . . and thinking . . . studying about things till he knew them, studying about ways till he found them, making things with his mind and his hand and his heart that the world knew were important, dreaming his dreams . . . and, yes, sometimes bowing, bowing and scraping and laughing, laughing easy at the white man, laughing easy at Mr. Poor White and Mr. Rich White, laughing loud at Mr. Negro, laughing belly laughs at Mr. Negro to hide his sorrow and his fear and his anger and his shame that nothing was due him.

Nobody told him for a long time that up in Washington he still had a bargain. Nobody told him up there were Nine Men who could read it. Had to find that out for himself. Even then . . . even then . . . it's a long way to Washington and it takes money, takes powerful money and time and courage to knock on the door of Nine Judges and ask them to read you your bargain, ask them to read it out loud, so everybody in the world can hear it. . . .

After a time Mr. Poor White got to studying. Seemed like things ought to be kind of different. Mighty fine to sit in the front seat by Mr. Rich White, mighty fine to turn round now and then and see the nigger right there on the back seat where you shoved him. But still, you ain't driving. Mr.

Rich White's driving, and you get restless, for it looks like he's driving down a road that goes nowhere, when you need to stop at the store to do some buying. Need to get flour and meat and milk for the younguns and shoes for the family and a new roof over your head and medicine for the baby, and a job that won't wear out tomorrow, and a few games to play with.

But Mr. Rich White says, "Can't stop now, better keep watching that nigger!—Is he still on the back seat, still there where you shoved him?"

"Yeah," you say, "he's still there."

"Well, what's the matter? Don't you like sitting up here on the front seat by me, don't you like that?"

"Yeah, I like that," you say, "but folks got to have things; folks can't keep on making out with what they have forever; seems like I oughta stop at the store and do some buying; seems like maybe you've taken a road that don't stop at stores," Mr. Poor White said suddenly.

"Listen," said Mr. Rich White, "you want me to let that stinking nigger come up here and sit with you? You want that? Want him to marry your sister?" And he slowed down as he said it.

"No," said Mr. Poor White, "reckon that ain't what I want, I couldn't stand that."

"Didn't think you could," said Mr. Rich White, speeding up a little as he drove on down the road that went nowhere.

Mr. Poor White kept studying. Wonder if he *was* up here, could the two of us turn that wheel a little way in my direction?

"I've heard tell," said Mr. Rich White as he drove on to nowhere, "of communist folks and cross-eyed liberals so low-down they'd associate with niggers just to get 'em into their unions. Ever know a white man low-down as that?"

"No," said Mr. Poor White, "never knowed a white man low-down as that."

"Brother," said the black man in the back seat (easy-like), "don't you think we could do it? Together we could do it?"

"Maybe," said Mr. Poor White (voice mighty easy), "maybe; but you couldn't come near me except in the union, you hear that?"

"Yessir," said the Negro, "I hear that."

The bargain was breaking. Mr. Rich White's and Mr. Poor White's bargain was breaking. Nobody knew how it happened, but they knew it. Breaking in slivers, sloughing in dry rot, and sometimes cracking with a terrible scream as of deep-rooted trees split by lightning.

Folks said it had to break, you ought to see that; times are changing, ways of making money are changing, the world is changing; things can't keep on forever in the old way.

But Mr. Rich White blamed it on the damyankee and the New Deal and the Communist and Mrs. Roosevelt and the Negro press and the social scientists and that little fellow in India and southern traitors and a crazy world that won't stop shrinking, and on his own sons and daughters and their mothers, who didn't seem to know that if you keep talking about the white primary, keep talking about equal education, keep talking about Negro health, keep talking about housing, keep talking about equal jobs and pay, keep talking about fourth-grade sardine-and-cracker culture, keep talking Christian brotherhood, the churches will begin to take brotherhood seriously and Mr. Poor White will keep filling his unions with niggers, keep right on filling them, making them bigger and stronger, and first thing you know he may not even *care* whether he's better than niggers! And then what about money and wages and jobs and hours and things like that! What about the thing you lost long time ago, so long ago in your childhood that you can't remember even what it was, but you keep on hunting it, hunting in your dreams, hunting day and night. . . . Don't they know you got to have *money* to find it! Don't they know things must stay as they are or you'll never find it!

"Let 'em talk," Something whispered. "Long as you have segregation none of these things can happen! Just keep saying *nothing can change it, nothing!* Make your sons and daughters say it and your newspapers say it and your politicians say it. The poor white will say it with you, for he's got to be better than something!"

"You still want to be better than the nigger?" asked Mr. Rich White.

"Yes," said Mr. Poor White, "I still want to be better than the nigger."

"See?" Something said.

"Yes, but why are so many folks against us! Everybody's against us. . . . The whole world! Even my own children," said Mr. Rich White.

"I'm for you," Something said, "and the southern politician's for you. And a lot of Yankee Republicans are for you. And there are a lot of people in Europe for you. A lot of folks are still for you everywhere. I'm for you—I'm always for the guy who wants to be first; I'm for the guy who loves his own image; I'm for the guy who rides the front seat, always the front seat, and won't let others ride with him."

"Who are you?"

"You know me . . . every man from the womb knows me until death stops the knowledge. But some won't make me a bargain. You did. Yes, you did and I'm for you. Who am I? Listen, I'll tell you. I'm that which splits a mind from its reason, that splits a soul from its conscience, a heart from its loving, a people from humanity. I'm the seed of hate and fear and guilt. You are its strange fruit which I feed on. . . ."

But Mr. Rich White and Mr. Poor White did not understand the words and turned from them.

"Listen," Something said, "nothing can change me, nor you. Nothing! Don't you remember?"

And now they felt the old familiar shadow pressing upon them. . . .

"None but the weak," said a Voice, "crave to be *better than*. None but the weak crave that. Strong men are satisfied with their own strength and their freedom. There is another way to make bargains. . . ."

"Who are you?"

"You've known me too, but you lost me. I am that which holds a mind together, which keeps a spirit from breaking, which makes a people human. I am the key that opens a locked door. I am the stone rolled away from a tomb. I'm just the guy who sits on the front seat and wants everybody to sit there with him. I'm that which you lost . . . and keep hunting. Why don't you find me?"

"Everybody hush talking!"

But the Voice would not hush. And sometimes it sounded as quiet and simple as Jesus; and sometimes as plain-written as the Bill of Rights; and sometimes it sounded like rain after a dry spell; and sometimes like your mother's step when you call her; and sometimes like a mind that has found itself; and sometimes like the Word that is God. And sometimes it sounded like a new song, made of all of these, of brotherhood and freedom and democracy and the Bill of Rights, yes, and sanity and science and love and integrity and laughter: a fine new hymn to the living the whole world is learning to sing.

"Come, sing it with us!"

Mr. Rich White and Mr. Poor White turned away. "We can't learn it," they whimpered; "we can't even carry its tune!"

"Don't listen," Something said, "don't listen. Remember your bargain, remember nothing can change it, nothing!"

They tried to remember. But suddenly they knew that this thing which held them so tightly in its beak and its claws was not their bargain with each other, for that was already breaking, they knew that; but the great death-bird and nothing could change it, nothing—unless they changed themselves. And the shadow fell closer and the claws and the beak sank deeper. . . .

⌐ 3 ⌐

Tobacco Road Is a Long Journey

NO WHITE southerners, rich or poor, ever sat down and wrote out this bargain as a creed to believe and to live by, or ever said aloud or whispered in their own minds all of it at one time, or ever faced in their hearts its full implications for people who claim to be Christian and democratic; for it grew on them, little by little. It was absorbed by them from their newspapers, from their friends' talk, in smoking compartments of trains, in wispy little odds and ends of jokes and rumor, from politicians' speeches and promises. They often contradicted it in their actions, they were inconsistent in expressing it in their talk, their Christian conscience sometimes made them deny it, their hearts sometimes refused to abide by it; for it was not an ideology cut and dried, a creed, handed down to them from police powers above as in Russia or from the authority of the church. It grew from bitter years when it was hard for the luckiest man in the devastated South to make a living, from hurt pride over having lost a war to the Yankee, from psychosexual insecurities that reached deep into childhood, from the aching need for a scapegoat (two were better),

from utter boredom and loneliness and an ignorance that
made a hodgepodge of ideas, and from the hideously seductive fact that for the few the bargain paid off in fabulous
profits and always—as in gambling—one hoped to be one
of the few.

It worked for a long time. Each "stood by" the other. When
the poor white lynched a Negro, the rich white protected
him in court; the preacher protected him in church; the
policeman looked away, the sheriff was easily intimidated,
the juries rarely convicted, and the newspapers were "reasonable." When unions came South and began to push southern industrialists, the poor white stood by the textile and
tobacco mills and fought the unions that had come South
to help him gain higher wages and better living conditions;
and fought the liberals who were trying to help the rural
whites secure better schools and housing and jobs and farms
of their own, and hospitals for their sick. It was hard for them
to believe—it is hard today for the rural southerner to believe—that unions are for them and to their advantage; they
still are "loyal" to the old bargain, and too, Negro-hating
has come now to be such a habit (like the taking of drugs)
that many would rather stay poor than give it up; and others
hope—those who go to the mills to work—that they can
have better wages by joining unions and still keep their
unions segregated.

It is equally hard for the rural white southerner to believe
that the southern liberals who champion their rights are not
"Communists." They call them "Communists" if they fight
demagoguery which devours the poor, if they work for
higher wages, if they defend human rights, if they oppose
war and segregation, if they believe in co-operatives and
freedom of conscience and speech which communism does
not believe in, and if they fight authoritarianism which is

the essence of communism. The rural white looks with suspicion on southern writers who, deeply loving the South where they were born and live, write honestly of it so that its people may gain insight into its vast needs. It is as irrational as hating a doctor for telling you that you are ill, as feeling insulted when he diagnoses your illness, but many southern whites react in this way, partly because of the bargain and partly because, under the authoritarian system of white supremacy twisted up with Christian fundamentalism, they have been taught to believe one is disloyal when one makes any criticism of things as they are, even when one criticizes great evil.

The political part of the bargain came out of the two groups' conflict with each other during the rise of populism. For a long time the planters had controlled the region's politics. There was the greedy carpetbag interim, the chaotic Reconstruction decade after the war when Yankee and Negro took over for a little; but the Compromise of 1876 eased this sound and fury and the dominant southern group had begun once more to "get things in hand," when out of the Midwest, like a cyclone, came the populist movement—a kind of common-man rural awakening. Southern politics has always bred the political opportunism that fattens on what is near at hand; so it was easy for men like Tom Watson of Georgia and Ben Tillman of South Carolina to come forward with demagogic glibness to "befriend" the rural whites. Things began to happen quickly after that. Mr. Rich White's politician voted the Negro en masse to stem the political rise of the "common people"; Mr. Poor White's politician caught on to the trick and voted the Negro himself when he had the power to do so and when he did not, slapped qualifications on law books to keep Negroes from voting at all. In retaliation Mr. Rich White's politician slapped on the poll tax not only to keep the poor white from voting freely but in order to buy up blocs of the poor whites' votes for his own use.

It was more of a battle than a bargain but nowhere was democracy an issue in the fight, as rarely has it been an issue in southern political campaigns since then. Both the Negro and the rural white lost, for the poll tax penalized the poor white man even more than it did the black man (who had already been deprived of the ballot by the grandfather clauses); and the total effect was to take away from both their sovereign right to vote.

The next step was the white primary, which was the means of reconciling the two white groups. After all, using the Negro vote against each other was playing with fire, they said; white folks had better stick together; poor folks and rich both have white skins and cannot afford to fight each other. And so they set up the white primary which was in effect an "election," held a few months before general election, in which only white members of the Democratic party—the only real party in the South—voted for the candidates. The white primary was the political bargain, the compromise by which southern rich and southern poor achieved "peace" and "unity" and made the South solid.

Through its means, not only unity but a political totalitarianism of immense power was achieved. It established the one-party system which has made and kept the South solid for seven decades. And, with the aid of the poll tax, reduced voting to a small fraction of the region's citizens of voting age.

But this bargain could never have been carried through had not another bargain been made with the North.

There are a thousand nuances of politics, business, personalities, and prejudice in this agreement known as the Compromise of 1876, but its basic result was to return white supremacy to the South eleven years after the war to free the slaves, in payment for political and economic concessions to the North.

What a tale of irony it is! Stripped to its bone the story is this:

After the Civil War when southerners were in panic because of the race disorders of Reconstruction, and northern interests were looking covetously at rich untapped resources of southern materials and markets and labor, and Republican and Democratic parties were in heated controversy over a national election, the Republicans, backed quietly by northern economic powers, agreed to let the southern Democrats manage the "Negro problem" in their own way if their spokesmen would accept the Republican candidate Hayes as President—though there was strong evidence that the Democratic Tilden had actually won the election. The South accepted. Hayes became President, Negroes became the white South's "problem," the Supreme Court drew the teeth from the Civil Rights Act, interpreting the Fourteenth Amendment to accord with this gentlemen's agreement, and suddenly new bright voices in the North began to drown out the old abolitionists' talk of human freedom by saying "the race problem is insoluble."

From 1877 to 1915 there was peace among white folks, North and South. It was not good form to talk of race problems. This white unity swelled into a riptide of stereotyped defenses that made thinking unnecessary. In southern and northern accents the proper answers were said: *The South understands the Negro. . . . After all, the Negro is only three hundred years out of the jungle. . . . Segregation is here to stay; it makes for peace for the races to be separated. . . . You can't change things overnight. . . . This is not the*

*right time. . . . These things have to be done by slow edu-
cation. . . . You can't legislate brotherhood. . . . After all,
now, would you want your sister. . . .*

The tide of white unity throughout our nation rose higher
and higher and did not begin to ebb until the year 1915
brought the Supreme Court's first no to white supremacy in
Dixie, in a decision which ruled unconstitutional the voting
requirements called "grandfather clauses" (which had been
set up in southern states to deprive Negroes of the ballot by
requiring proof that their grandfathers had "voted"; in other
words, had not been in slavery). But it turned very slowly.
After that one decision, the Supreme Court made no other in
favor of civil rights for more than a decade. And, until the
New Deal, our national government was loath to break the
old bargain.

In the meantime, Negroes had organized in protest against
the region-wide discrimination and with the assistance of
white friends in the North began a dramatic defense of their
legal rights both in the courts and in books and papers and
forums. Though there were northerners who stubbornly
held to the bargain, repeating old rusty clichés that I have
heard all of my life in Dixie, there were others who began to
protest this betrayal of democracy; and there were southerners who turned away from the old segregation creed that
they had memorized in babyhood and refused to bow down
to southern tradition. Questions were asked. Consciences,
North and South, grew more and more uneasy. Old men on
the Court died. New ones, more just, took their places. Decision after decision of the U.S. Supreme Court in favor of
civil rights, books, poems, protest movements, began to melt
the deep-freeze in men's minds in which human rights had
been stored away.

But, in Congress, the gentlemen's agreement held firm.

Southern congressmen, elected by a handful of people, with no Negro constituency (until recently), resolutely maintained their collaboration with northern reactionaries in matters of race and labor, though their speech was heavy with invectives against the new "Yankee interference" which became now a real threat to their bargain that had been profitable so long. (It is a nice little paradox that southern Democrats can today maintain this political bargain with northern Republicans only by holding on to a one-party system which keeps the Republican party out of the South. The whole business takes on a fine Alice-in-Wonderland flavor.)

The South has been kept "solid" a long time by this one-party system which depends for its staying power on the highly emotional beliefs in states' rights and segregation. Such a one-party system, as we knew long before we began to observe its dynamics in Russia, makes it impossible for the people to decide by ballot any major issue for the simple reason that these issues are inevitably obscured by the "line." Political campaigns have been, therefore, mainly battles for power between two factions of the same party, neither of which dares deviate from these basic beliefs.

Sometimes a campaign begins with a "safe" issue such as economy in government, public roads, or freedom of the university system from political restraint, or even sometimes with as "controversial" a matter as the white primary, or the county unit system. Inevitably, in the fight for votes— whether the issue is close to or remote from "race"—the candidate closest to the rural people will use the "Negro question" as an irresistible weapon, plunging it into his opponent by accusing him of being in favor of "social equality." The farcical battle begins. In reply, his opponent will declare in righteous indignation that he too believes in segregation, he

too believes in states' rights, he too is as loyal as any son of
the Confederacy to southern tradition. But sometimes, if he
is a decent person, he will add that he does want the Negro
to have justice. That gives the heckling candidate the advantage, and now he redoubles his accusations until the air
is full of incredible phrases about "menace," "our white
women," "enforced intimate relations," "co-education of the
races," and so on. Whatever the original issue was that might
have given the electorate a small basis on which to make a
rational choice, it is now forgotten. In an atmosphere highly
charged, the people go to the ballot boxes and vote for the
man who seems most able to play on their secret anxieties.

The accused candidate—no matter how liberal he is in
private—is faced, in such an issue, with only two alternatives
that he and his political advisers will consider: one is to meet
the accusations in dignified silence; the other is to reaffirm
his loyalty to southern tradition, to repeat and keep repeating the creed of segregation and thus try to convince the
electorate that he is as ardent a white supremacist as his opponent. Neither works well with the people, for he is on the
defensive and a man on the defensive does not cut a fine political figure—at least with country folks. Secretly they are
also ashamed that he is unwilling to come out and take a
stand for what is right. For they know in their hearts that
this question of human rights is far more important, far more
basic, far more "rational" than the issue of roads or economy
and so on. Were he to turn around and really fight, were he
to declare in words of honest eloquence his belief in human
rights, were he to make a tight case against segregation that
would not only appeal to logical minds but light a candle in
men's murky imaginations, he would swing all the decent
voters in the state to his side. But the politicians in a southern

state will not gamble on there being a majority of decent
people, and this third alternative is never tried. With profound cynicism they play the game as if no one can be elected
in Dixie on a democratic, Christian platform.

In my lifetime, there has never been a campaign in Georgia
where any major candidate took a stand against segregation.
Carmichael, in 1946, while campaigning for the governor-
ship, declared his opposition to the white primary and put up
a good fight, but he was careful not to express opposition to
segregation. The one exception we have is the young
preacher, Joe Rabun, who ran as an independent candidate
in the campaign of 1948 and made nonsegregation the major
plank in his platform, but he had no backing from the liberal
group, no money, no experience in politics. He had only
courage. Though most southern liberals would say, I think,
that his race did more harm than good, I like to believe that
his function in that iniquitous campaign was analogous to the
job of a paratrooper or commando in the war who, knowing
he is expendable, goes ahead in order to open the way for
those who follow him. From this point of view Rabun made
a real contribution, which the next liberal candidate in
Georgia will undoubtedly profit from.

It is not only the bargaining away of one's integrity in order to be "useful" that disturbs me about political campaigns,
it is the liberals' forfeiture of their opportunity to carry to the
people our democratic beliefs. The people are listening as
they never listen at other times, minds are ready to receive
and ponder what their candidates have to say. The southern
conscience, so long deprived of nourishment, is hungry for
words that recreate the dream of the importance in this
world of the free human being.

But what do our people hear?

In one campaign, not many years ago, they heard this:

White-Supremacy Candidate: As long as I am your Governor the
Jim Crow law will be preserved. As long as I am your Governor no Negro foreman will give orders to white men and
women in the mills of this state.

Liberal Candidate: If a nigger ever tried to get into a white
school in my part of the state, the sun would never set on his
head. And we wouldn't be running to the Governor or the
State Guard to get things done, either.

White-Supremacy Candidate: For my part, I am proud to be
called the champion of White Supremacy.

Liberal Candidate: This state is governed by white people and
always will be governed by white people.

White-Supremacy Candidate: Sure . . . the nigger has a place.
And that place is at the back door. There's no other place for
him.

Liberal Candidate: There is not a decent white man or woman
in our state who believes in educating whites and Negroes in
the same schools. There is not a decent white man or woman
here who believes in social equality among white and blacks.

And when this campaign was over, the Negro was still in
the South, the white man was still in the South, and both
were bruised and burnt to the bone by racial hate and fear.

Who is going to stop it, as long as the southerners in politics feel compelled to deny their real beliefs, and newspaper
editors feel a terrible necessity to call "fools" and "fanatics"
those who take a stand against segregation? Every honest
politician, every honest editor, is deeply troubled by this
moral dilemma. He knows in his heart that there are times
when he has surrendered his integrity to southern tradition
in as bending a way as a Russian surrenders his integrity to
the Politburo. And he apologizes for it in the same way a
Communist does by saying that ends justify means, that

there is no other way to "be useful to the South" except by betraying one's deepest beliefs. And sometimes he turns bitterly on "idealists" who question his "realism."

Southern tradition may be only a ghost stalking our land, while the Politburo is a police authority with real live guns, but both have the power, by the use of fear, to take from men their freedom to do right.

It is hard to decide which is more harmful to men's morals, the liberal or reactionary, in this confused South.

The reactionary candidate, while usually not disturbed by such a spiritual conflict, having killed his dream so long ago that he cannot remember having possessed it, rarely hates or fears Negroes; yet without one scruple he will plan a campaign deliberately to arouse the race-sex anxieties of the ignorant whites. In speeches and writings he will deliberately dehumanize the Negro race, deliberately play up sexual fears, deliberately wear down the poor white's belief in human decency until, released from the constraint of conscience by the hysteria which the demagogue has incited in them, these confused people will do violent acts against any individual or group who is different from them, having been taught that any one "different" is their mortal enemy. After each gubernatorial campaign in Georgia, we have a wave of lynchings and cross burnings and terroristic activities—not because of the few who dare to affirm human rights and dignity and brotherhood, but because of the millions who deny these truths by their silence while race-bigotry and white-supremacy words are chanted sometimes over radio and in newspaper, more often in front of courthouses, day after day. Newspapers become so confused that even the more liberal among them actually believe a denunciation of segregation will "incite violence" and insist that affirmations of human rights can "only do harm." They seem to have forgot that words can arouse a man's conscience as well as his baser passions, and that conscience in sane people is a determining factor in behavior; instead they treat the southern public as if it were either a moral moron or mentally ill.

After the poll tax and white primary laws were passed in the troubled days of our fathers the rest of the Jim Crow statutes were put quickly on the states' law books. Beginning in 1890, most of them were passed in less than two decades. White and Colored signs went up over doors and stayed there. Railroad stations, rest rooms, drinking fountains were labelled. A South mushroomed in strange duality; a sin and its shadow crept over the land. White church—colored church; white school—colored school; white toilet—colored toilet; white waiting room—colored waiting room. In this region of bleak want and poverty, the cost of maintaining white civilization mounted higher and higher though costs were not doubled. No: for Mississippi spent annually on education for the white child in 1945–46, $75.19, for the colored child $14.74; Georgia spent $82.57 for white, $31.14 for colored; South Carolina spent $100.38 for white and $39.64 for colored.

From 1890 on, *white-colored-white-colored* grew into a regional anthem that swells when tensions come, diminishes when tensions go, but there is always chanting. . . . Minds and hearts were aroused by fear and guilt, political greed, and sadistic sex fantasies that spiralled higher and higher. Almost anything could happen and much did. The Atlanta riot in 1906 . . . more and more lynchings of more and more sadistic nature, more white women succumbing to fantasies that they had been raped and sometimes there were actual rapings . . . more fantastic rumors and gruesome tales of brutality. Although 3,148 lynchings took place in the South from 1882 to 1946, no member of a lynch mob was given a death sentence or life imprisonment. Only 135 persons in the entire United States (according to records of years 1900–1946, during which time almost 3,000 lynchings took place) have been convicted of being members of lynch mobs.

The responsible, educated, well-to-do group who still thought of themselves as dominant (or hoped they still were) did not know how to stop this Frankenstein, created of poverty, fear, ignorance, guilt, political greed, and crazed by the drug of white supremacy. Nor could they confess to themselves their big role in creating the monster. So they turned away and laid down a heavy smoke screen of silence over the South's racial tensions. It became taboo to talk of these problems; bad form to question; bad ethics to discuss the issues in the newspapers or write about them in books. They hoped silence would cure what intelligence and good will felt helpless to combat. If one did not mention these ghosts, maybe the ghosts would just go away. If everyone would only tiptoe . . . and whisper . . . and not talk aloud about human freedom and human dignity and human rights, maybe you could keep from stirring up violence. If segregation were never mentioned and were simply accepted as something unchangeable—like volcanoes and hurricanes and droughts—maybe everybody, even the Negro, would finally bow down before it. If we'll all be very very quiet and never question the *status quo* in any way, maybe some day we shall wake up and find this hell we are living in is only a bad dream.

I suppose this state of mind—which began slowly to change two decades ago, though revived now by each political campaign—was a massive schizophrenic withdrawal before trouble too immense to accept. I remember, as a child, hearing relatives and friends say complacently, that there was no Negro problem, it was all settled. I remember that, like *sex*, the word *segregation* was not mentioned in the best circles. Everything was firmly shut away. When one came in contact with a Negro one knew, one was courteous, smiling, a bit condescending—as grown folks often are to children. That is all. One's mind refused all questions. Everything was insoluble; therefore everything was settled.

By 1908, most southern states had the movements and habits of their people well covered by laws that made rigid the avoidance customs which had appeared here and there but which, gradually, our people might have outgrown (and many, I hope, would never have accepted) as more understanding of human relations was acquired, and as a little prosperity eased the widespread insecurity.

Jim Crow was a political trick in the beginning, but a trick that fitted like a glove on the white South's greedy, guilty hand. It paid politicians and still pays them the highest profits they receive down here. But it paid men even more in economic power—North and South—for it gave them an irrational weapon by which to weaken labor and to control the politicians who in turn control the rural votes, though the law of diminishing returns has set in concerning its use now, and many shrewd industrialists realize it. But these laws paid most profitably of all in closing off the conscience to questions. They hid so much. They justified so much. And they gave troubled people the final answer, "You can't break a law, can you?"

People said it and sighed in relief for the state had now decided what their own Christian conscience, for decades, had been unwilling to decide. They did not say, "But these statutes have made legal a way of life that is wrong, that destroys personality of white and colored, and makes freedom a grim joke and religion an empty piece of hypocrisy." No, they rejoiced that "once more they were led like sheep."

They were exhausted from war, worn-out from a conflict with the North in which, as is true today, right and wrong were inextricably mingled on both sides; they were without learning and bereft of fun; they were already loaded with guilt, and they gave up—as people all over the world today are giving up under pressures too heavy for them—and giving up, they submitted to an authority outside their own minds. And the North turned its head away. . . .

This was the "reconciliation" between northern reactionaries and their southern fellow travelers; this was the "unity" in Congress—acclaimed so loudly—when men without integrity made deals that were profitable to both northern and southern economic and political interests and highly unprofitable for American democracy. And this was the beginning of an authoritarian regime in the South during which state, church, home, school, and courts (contrary to the teachings of Jesus, of science and democracy) taught or defended the ideology of white supremacy and the constellation of skin-color-purity concepts that fixed and supported it and kept the mind of the people from questioning its "truth," and set up segregation as the South's highest law.

It was possible to do this, not only because of the stress and strains our people were weakened by, but because our minds were already split, our psychic energies divided, our consciences so troubled by anxieties given us as children that we could not concern ourselves with the rational needs of other men or even our own.

And now today, the old dominant white group fears these poorer rural whites, knowing at last that in the bargain it gave them control not only of the Negro but of southern culture also; that now with the ballot these whites, kept in ignorance and poverty so long, cut off for two centuries from the streams of scientific knowledge and world changes, have the power to make decisions affecting everyone's future not only in the South but throughout our nation.

And the poorer whites fear the old dominant white group, dimly sensing—though they do not know how or why—that powerful rich folks have kept millions in poverty and ignorance little better than peonage in exchange for this "right" to keep the Negro "in his place"; and while they still believe he should be kept there, just as simply and surely as they believe in God, yet they realize that they have been cheated of something and in their confusion they turn to demagogues who make them false promises, though these demagogues are supported by the same powerful group of rich men who have been feeding the rural white the drug of white supremacy in lieu of real food since the 1870's. And while these two groups are in false battle with each other— like the medievalists pitting one epicycle against another, unaware that science has made all epicycles unreal—the Negro group is fearing both poor and rich white, who have done Negroes so much harm for so long. All—rich, and poor, and Negro—lean on confusion and hate as a crutch for their weakness, having no longer the bargains to lean on, and fearing democracy as a way of life too hard for weak men to live up to.

The bargain is broken and all groups know it. There are no longer even these three groups, for now labor has broken the lines of race, and the liberals (rich and poor, city and rural), and church women white and colored, have broken the lines of color and class, so there is confusion everywhere; and no one knows who the real "enemy" is, or with whom he should align himself.

Once more in the South, the ancient fable is told of the sale of a birthright for a mess of pottage, the old legend repeated again and again in Bible and history book and myth of man's greed destroying him. And in northern accent it is told also, for the national Compromise of 1876, the bargain the North made with the South, is a part of the same old story. The South bargained away its economic resources to the North and the North bargained away its rightful share of power in Congress to the South through the poll tax and white primary which its compromise helped bring about. These two ballot restrictions made it possible for southern congressmen to be elected sometimes by as little as five per cent of the potential voters of their districts; and once elected, they can stay securely in Congress, term after term, until seniority bequeaths them the most influential and powerful offices in Senate and House. Today, these southerners, by means of filibuster and compromise with Republican reactionaries, are making decisions affecting not only American lives but the future of the whole world.

Tobacco Road is a long dark journey . . . leading from eroded little cotton and corn and tobacco patches through the South to Washington, on to Wall Street, to Europe, to Israel, to India and China, to the days of medievalism and back again to slavery, to state capitals, to Main Street, to Moscow, to ballot box, to the bank, to church and courthouse, to a man's childhood and his deepest fears . . . curving and twisting from one to another endlessly.

⌐ 4 ⌐

Southern Waste

THE GREAT waste of talent and imagination and brains and integrity that resulted from our way of life has been the South's greatest loss.

Bad health and poverty took a heavy toll of energy from our people, but there were few outlets for the energy left, few ways of salvaging restless fantasies in word or paint, sculpture or music or dance or in scientific inquiry.

The rigors of pioneer life had much to do with this impoverishment. In early rural society no one owned a "picture" or "statue," rarely a book unless he were of the small wealthy group. There were no art galleries, no public libraries, and little serious music. There was no knowledge of these things, nor money to buy them with, nor time for creating them, for hands and minds were needed for another purpose. They were needed to chop down trees, fight wild animals, break a trail through a swamp, outwit Indians, build houses, open up fields; and this work satisfied most men's psychic needs.

In such a culture, the boy who withdrew with a chunk of clay and a dream and fashioned them into a piece of sculpture, or messed around painting or writing stories, was called a plain fool. Dimly folks sensed, too, that his emotional needs were stronger than theirs, that things were happening inside of him that "decent folks should be ashamed of" and they were ashamed of him—in the same way that they were ashamed of the insane member of the family or the daughter who became pregnant outside of marriage.

It was not strange for them to believe in the immorality of the creative process, for their preachers—from circuit-rider to revivalist—had warned them that art, decoration, dancing, novels, and curiosity pandered to the evil in men's natures. Critical intelligence was "wrong"—both Catholic and Protestant churches had long opposed the new learning; science was "wrong"; curiosity, already dulled by the suppression of the child's early explorations of his small world, was "wrong."

The frustration and guilt that resulted from these restrictions sometimes put a spell on hands and mind so that they could not again connect with those daydreams out of which art comes, or with those first questions of the child that are the seeds of mature inquiry. And once locked up, it was not an easy thing to free them again.

A heavy pall had fallen across our spirits; so many little brightnesses of life were banned; so many easements forbidden. In my childhood, the wearing of jewelry was opposed by many Methodist ministers who quoted the Discipline rebukingly to those of their congregation who wore what they called "sinful baubles." "Painting of the face" and lipstick were frowned upon. Smoking is still a greater sin in many religious southerners' minds than segregation, which is rarely thought of as a sin by these strict people. Just as a patient, suffering from melancholia, refuses to "look pretty" or to wear becoming clothes or spend money for pleasure or do anything that might be fun because he "doesn't deserve it," rural and small-town people seemed to feel that they could not permit themselves any pleasures but eating—as if in deep penance for a more cherished sin which they could not give up or had committed so long ago that they could not remember it. And not wanting to remember, it was wise not to question one's self too closely.

There is much that reminds one of mental illness in this catalog of sins. It was so compulsive, so without humor. When we remember that our forefathers accepted slavery and that our people now accept gross racial discrimination and acute poverty and disease without letting these evils enter the region of "right" and "wrong," it becomes apparent that the morals of the South have been for too many only a mass cleansing of hands.

Aggression, when not expended against the family, was accepted by this troubled conscience. Wasting of land, wasting of natural resources, lawbreaking, vigilante groups, bootlegging of whiskey in prohibition counties, group violence, fist-fights, became southern characteristics. This acceptance of violence has piled up troubling statistics which tell us that the southern region has proportionately the most murders, as well as the most churches, the most poverty, the highest rate of illiteracy, lowest wages, poorest health, most eroded soil of any section of our nation.

As skilled use of the hands in aggression became more and more valued in this pioneer-planter culture, skilled use of the hands in work was increasingly looked down upon. Men who worked with their hands were depersonalized in this rural region of poverty, where only the white-collar workers were esteemed and especially the professional man and the man who did not work at all. You paid off the "hands," white and black, on Saturday; you put the "hands" to work on Monday morning.

I have sometimes thought that the rural people's fear of unions springs not alone from their fear of giving up their individualism, but from the fear that if one joins the union and becomes identified with "labor," one will surrender one's chance of becoming a "gentleman" who will no longer work with his hands.

Of the varied manifestations of the stresses in our culture, this fear of hands used creatively and the acceptance of hands that destroy seem to me most revealing. Men have grown afraid of their own human stature and of that which contributed so much to creating it.

Hands—that have reached for the stars and grubbed in the dirt, that have built a fire . . . that have carved fantasies of wood and stone and made clay into immortal images, that have painted pictures which can never be wiped off of man's memory, fashioned instruments and played music on them, pounded and stroked and molded and broken clay and metal and stone and wood . . . that have caressed and killed the human body . . . that have built great cities, planted vast fields, mined the earth and formed delicate, lovely gardens—now, in angry despair, destroying thousands of years of their own creations! One wonders when mankind will again honor them and put them back at their rightful work.

The colonials of Maryland, Virginia, and the Carolinas, who in early days set cultural levels which later the more crude and exploitative planter of the Deep South tried to identify with, placed little more value on the artist and the creative process than did the pioneer and "poor white" and lower-South Methodist and Baptist.

Though they hung many paintings—usually their own family's portraits—in their drawing rooms, this upper-South aristocracy valued the esthete rather than the creator, taste rather than truth, erudition rather than critical intelligence. The creative process was neither intuitively cherished as an emotional safety valve nor prized as the means of symbolizing men's important feelings about life. They, too, with all their surface sophistication, feared their fantasy life as much as did po' folks. The dread of the unconscious is no respecter of classes and—as is the way of the Anglo-Saxon—nearly everyone preferred to keep a safe distance from the profound depths of his own or another's nature.

But beautiful things were valued. Portraits in oils; furniture made by fine cabinetmakers; spinets and crystal chandeliers from Europe; rugs from France and the Near East; china, silver, old vases and clocks from England and the Orient; and hooked rugs of the Piedmont region, found their way during the 18th and early 19th centuries into tide-river homes stretching from Virginia to South Carolina to New Orleans and up the river to the more fabulously elegant homes in the delta. And today, these Colonial and pre-Civil War possessions are valued so much as symbols of a way of life which the few lived with grace and the many wistfully identify with, that a number of old southern homes are maintained, like mausoleums, and opened at stated intervals for the devout to visit. These pilgrimages seem to pay those who organize them, and the pilgrims (from North and South) seem to receive commensurate returns if one can judge by their dreamy-eyed stares at all this antebellum grandeur.

As cotton slipped across the land, as slaveholdings grew larger and the rich black fields of the lower South opened

up, and a new kind of pioneering took hold of minds, men
became too poor or too rich, too tired or too greedy, to
develop the resources of their own intellect and spirit. The
culture brought over from England to the tideland edges
of the South never flowered as in New England but wilted
and finally shriveled. So that at the time of the Civil War,
there were fine possessions but no art in the South; a few
libraries but no critics and writers, a little tinkly music but
no composers of importance. Planter families were riding
to hounds, drinking mint juleps and dancing, and hotly
arguing states' rights and their moral right to hold human
beings in slavery. Such a mood was not conducive to reading, but those who, in spite of it all, loved books were reading the Greek and Latin classics, committing to memory
Horace and Ovid, holding to these ancient writers as if to
a crumbling shore, unable to explore the deeps of their own
contemporary world, unwilling perhaps to make contact
with it. And the poorer families were spelling out the war
posters which were recruiting soldiers for the new Confederacy.

After the war, the wealthy who survived, either as the
old planter who held on or the new planter who took over,
lived much as before, though for a time more frugally. Their
sons spent winters in Paris and Italy, a few turned into book-
worms as had their uncles or fathers, reading and re-reading
the classics, thinking themselves learned because minds
blotted up so easily words which long ago were torn in
anguish or wisdom from another's heart and intelligence.
And, here and there, youngsters with more vitality and curiosity turned to southern journalism, hoping to find there
what they hungered for. But most of the South during those
hard decades was not reading at all. Those who read casually, turned away from everything that did not give them

comfort; for evil things were happening in Dixie and most southerners wanted to believe—they *had* to believe—that this evil was not of their making. Only books that convinced them of their blamelessness for the blackness of their times were acceptable.

In nearly two hundred years of white southern culture there was not one artist or critic or poet or dramatist or musician or writer (if we except Poe) produced here who was comparable to his contemporaries in Europe. Only in the past three decades have we had novelists like Thomas Wolfe and Faulkner and Evelyn Scott, of more than minor worth. Even now, much of our best talent goes into what F. L. Lucas calls "stained-glass writing," which shuts out the glare of the turmoil in man's soul and his world, seducing the feelings with its wondrous little patterns of words that block off insight carefully and graciously.

Writers became too subdued by the white Christian supremacy system, too overwhelmed by its luxury and poverty, to rebel and to write of life as they saw it around them and people as they knew them to be. And sometimes, alas, they no longer could see or know, having closed their eyes and mind. Instead, in devotion or despair, they wrote down the official daydream that the southern authoritarian system wanted the world to think our life was. This conspiracy of blindness, this collaboration with authority, entered into at first voluntarily but later made obligatory by custom, closed a heavy door on the mind and the senses. People knew so much that they dared not speak of aloud. They realized intuitively so much that they could not convince even themselves was the truth. They dreamed so many dreams that they feared, if written or put in color or clay, would seem to the people they loved to be terrifying nightmares, and to those whom they did not know but with whom they had identified so profoundly would seem an act of treason. So, in the way of Russia's writers and artists today, southern writers and artists created the official version or did not create at all. Few, almost none, were willing to undergo the public abuse and social rejection that usually followed disloyalty to southern tradition. (There was in the South no regional or state government with the power to banish such an artist or critic but there were—there still are—neighbors and newspapers and the Klan who could make life not worth the living.) Horace Kallen's depiction, in *Art and Freedom,* of the artist as one who stoutly maintains his right to be different, carrying gaily and gallantly the banners of freedom down through the centuries, reserving always the right to stay in bondage to his own daydreams and not those of any power or tradition or state, is an artist that the South rarely saw until the last few years.

Our southern artist was more likely, in the old days, to be a lady embroidering a pin cushion or painting flowers on velvet. Our poets were sometimes gentle souls like Lanier, but rarely did one of them put other than his carefully self-censored thoughts on paper, sifting them through layers of taboos and proprieties and decorums. Little appeared in print that could not be read as an inspirational thought at family prayers which many southerners had each morning.

The few artists who dared mess around in public with paints were usually looked upon as "abnormal"—effeminate if men, masculine if women. The men of science and the critics were treated with a bit more respect by being called "anti-Christ," as are psychoanalysts and even social scientists today by many southerners. A boy who was a pianist had to endure the worst treatment of all, being called "sissy" and whispered of as a "hermaphrodite," and was so terrorized by tongues that there were few who survived the ordeal without mental breakdown. And this continued until the day of swing orchestras and popular band leaders who, whatever their artistic achievements, made life more bearable at last for men musicians in Dixie.

Feelings and attitudes are changing today. Artists and writers are beginning to create their own dreams and not the official daydream. Critics are beginning to speak their real beliefs and not those of southern tradition, though they find it sometimes rough going among the homefolks.

But for nearly two centuries, white supremacy and Christian asceticism of a crude naïve kind combined with isolation and poverty to destroy the vast talent that was dormant among white southerners, leaving our region as bereft of art, music and dance, ideas and books, as any group of civilized people probably in all the world.

It is one of many paradoxes of our way of life that among the dominant free, talent was so bound by anxiety that it could not be released, while among the slaves and the segregated, talent burst forth spontaneously.

Though this talent found varied outlets in the work of the artisan, the creative activities of Negroes were for a long time limited to what could be done with their bodies for that was all they had to do with.

Their songs and dance, their spirituals and their jazz, were welcomed by all people of the Western world as hungrily as an undernourished child eats candy. For these creations, this poignancy of song, this access to sorrow and abandon to instinctual rhythms, met a deeper need than most realized, reuniting us with a part of ourselves so long hidden away in shame.

But we wanted none of the Negro's brains. We rejected

the intellectual richness that piled higher and higher in the minds of those who acquired learning. Negro social scientists and physicists, writers, scholars in the fields of law, medicine, and chemistry we tried to ignore. And back of them the procession of young trained minds, now a hundred thousand or more, we would not look at. Instead, we shut this wealth away on the campuses of Negro colleges which most southerners have never visited and many do not know exist.

There are fine buildings, there are beautiful grounds, and good libraries; there are as well-trained faculties as in most white southern colleges, and the young people in them are healthy and eager and perhaps of a higher intelligence level than the average in white schools; but there is, even so, something about a segregated college that reminds me too much of a mental hospital, for the people inside are shut away from communication with the rest of America's people—not because they are ill, but because the culture outside has lost its health.

I remember, once, when I was on such a campus. The young secretary of the president of the college was showing me the grounds. She was a lovely thing to look at, quiet, poised, and I found her face more interesting than buildings and spacious gardens. We walked near the entrance that led to the street and stood, watching a streetcar pass by toward the "white" section of town. And then we turned back toward the library. I said, "It is beautiful in here, peaceful, quiet. I find it hard to remember the world out there that I will go back to tomorrow." She did not answer for a moment, then she said softly, "I wish I never had to go out there, even to shop. I would like never to go. In here, one forgets; you can believe you are real, a person. You go out there and they tear it off of you, your belief in yourself as something good, they tear it off in five minutes. It doesn't take much, a word you hear a man say, a glance, some one draws aside, that is all; a clerk in a store asks you your first name as if she cannot otherwise sell you a pair of shoes. Little things. . . . And suddenly you are an untouchable. In here . . . sometimes for a month I do not remember those people, outside."

I wonder which of those liberals who say they believe it could tell her that segregation is "best" for her and her people, that it is "here to stay" and no one should "try to change it." Sometimes I wonder if those who have *entrée* everywhere know what the feeling is that a sensitive, intelligent person has who is set apart; and if they are aware of how segregation has made their own personalities small and tight and their hearts so dull.

In these schools are faculties made up in large part of brilliant, sensitive, talented, Negro men and women, many of whom possess the highest kind of scholastic and scientific training. Sometimes a fine white scholar, like Dr. Robert Park, who was at Fisk University for so long, will be found in a department. Nearly always, there is a scattering of white missionaries who with good motives and sometimes good brains, have dedicated their lives to the "betterment" of the Negro race.

Of these latter, a heavy price is exacted by the white community for their missionary zeal. Though the attitude is now slowly changing, these white teachers, many from the North, a few of the South, have been outcasts in their southern communities. I have been told by them that they have lived on the campus of a Negro college for twenty years without receiving a social invitation from the white Christian community. Yet these same communities send missionaries to China and India and Africa to save the "heathen," and graciously entertain these missionaries (even the ones who have been to Africa) upon their return. It is a thing to ponder. Africa . . . full of white Americans who in their hearts wanted to do something to help the Negro in the South and dared not, and turned instead to foreign missions, finding it easier to brave distance and disease, tropical heat, jungle, plains, loneliness, than to brave the hostility of their own people.

Not long ago a young missionary wrote me this letter:

> I wanted to stay in the South and help rid it of lynching and segregation. That is what I really wanted to do. But there was Mother . . . you know how disgraced she would have felt had I stayed and helped here. She would have died if she had seen me eating with a Negro. . . . But she is proud of me now, going to Africa as a missionary. She calls me her "missionary daughter" and gave a party last week in honor of my going. Mother's friends said they were proud of me too—going so far away to help Christianize Africa. And the president of the U. D. C. in our town is giving me a party next week; she's proud of me too. I am the only one ashamed.
>
> Tonight I feel like a coward for I know I am needed here. My boat sails in two weeks. Maybe in some way over there I can show a little courage. I don't think I'm afraid for myself . . . it's Mother. I love her; I can't hurt her. How do you learn to hurt the people you love, even when you know they're wrong, for something you know is right? That is so hard.

Yes, that is so hard. And it is a hard thing too that the South has wasted this fine moral fervor by forcing it out of our region, saying there is no room for it here.

Of the Negro colleges, each campus is a little different: the warmth of a generous personality, the releasing effect of one man with a big sense of humor, the bruising power of one man's profound scepticism, the illuminating glow from one giant imagination, the poison freed by one man's deep hate—such intangibles change the atmosphere of a campus, even from year to year, making it impossible to talk as if Negro colleges in the South are alike. But all of them are alike in that their students and their faculties are cut off from the main-stream of American society; and all are alike in that the human beings in them feel psychologically shunned by the rest of America; and all have the certainty that whenever their graduates leave their "retreat," they will be thrust out into a hostile society that will have doors for them to walk through and buildings that they must keep out of, libraries that they cannot use, research departments in schools of higher education closed to them; and few positions for which they will be eligible because of their color.

There have been excellent books written on southern waste of soil and manpower and forest and minerals, but the wasting away of the nature of man has been the South's greatest loss.

Body and mind, imagination and conscience, dreams and the skill of hands, have washed away in the gullies made by anxiety and fear and hate and greed. What a thin empty shell we have left!

For so long we were concerned not with the growth of children and the welfare and health of the human race and the quality of our relationships one with another, but with the mouth and the genitals; the body had become in a curious, inverse way, the center of our moral universe, around which anxieties and guilt hovered. Nothing but ourselves seemed important. Tenderness, pity, concern for others were driven from our minds by guilt and fear. To punish was so much easier than to understand; to push out of sight so much more comfortable than to accept and make room for. Sin-centered, we had no concern for the happiness of others.

This narcistic flight of conscience, participated in for centuries by Western church and Western culture, is one of the most interesting happenings of human history. Everything that had to do with the body was labeled "sacred" or "profane": sacred and profane love, sacred and profane food; certain areas of the body were profane, others sacred. Drinking, smoking, no matter how moderate, were profane; eating, no matter how excessive or how callously done while others starved, was sacred; sex experiences, outside of marriage, no matter how tender and responsible, were profane; sex experiences in marriage, no matter how cruel and sadistic and destructive to human personality, were sacred.

It is not too difficult to see how possible, how logical, was the transition to "sacred" and "profane" people according to criteria as infantile as skin color and as primitive as "blood," and how easy it was to set up taboos concerning eating with or marrying "profane" people, or even coming in contact with them in public places. Narcissus, not God, had become our Judge and Law Maker. What the child had been compelled to cast away returned to the man as a burden too heavy to bear.

Perhaps the first deep chasm in our Western culture was dug, the first separation made, long ago, when the church officially proclaimed asceticism the "superior" life. Perhaps it was this degradation of the human body, this segregation of inferior flesh from superior soul, this splitting of sacred from profane love—weakening love until it is no match for hate—that was the primal schizophrenic act that set the strange pattern which has caught up the Western world now in the stiff measures of what sometimes seems a dance of death. Perhaps this profound conflict in Christian religion —the Christ holding up an ideal of love, of brotherhood, of rich warm human relationships, and the church loading the conscience with too much guilt for men ever to feel such love or to form such relationships—first split Western man's acts from his ideals, for only by such a rift in his mind could he hold on to these mutually destroying beliefs and give them both his loyalty, as he has tried desperately to do ever since.

I do not know the answers to these speculations, but I think we need to know. It has been too easy, for the past hundred years, for that magic word *economic* to slam and lock doors that have been banging in men's troubled minds so long.

The South, a tortured fragment of Western culture, simply regressed under its heavy strains to a more crude and naïve expression of these splits than did the rest of white Christendom—until Germany with her logic and scientific learning and lack of moral ambivalence carried to its final insane ends this paranoid system of separating the sacred from the profane among men.

These forces, these strains, piled one on another through long weary years, made the whole South sick but took a heavier toll of the poorer whites than richer whites because of their greater vulnerability. Not because they were "worn-out stock," as their richer kinfolks said, or "degenerates," as others have said, were these people lazy and shiftless. We know this now. They were "lazy and shiftless" from malaria, heat, decades of malnourishment, and a slave-making poverty. They were lazy from loneliness, and darkness, and the false sense of sin which their culture had laid on them, and from taking the drug of white supremacy which destroyed their minds and integrity. A few were lazy, God bless them, because the sun was warm, any shelter would do, and the fishing was good! And some were not lazy at all but worked from "can to can't" trying to make a living on submarginal land that had no living left in it; while others worked as hard on deep rich black land, after the Civil War, with no chance to succeed in the meteoric American manner under a sharecropping system of agriculture that averaged in the thirties a family income of $309 a year.

Having so few acceptable outlets for aggressions and anxieties that piled up heavily on mind, body and soul, they were compelled to turn these feelings back upon themselves or those near them, until sometimes they destroyed their own or someone else's mental or physical health. Feuds in the mountains, making of moonshine, drinking hard liquor, hunting and killing of animals, lynching a Negro, political hate-sex fests, wondrous streaks of corny wry shrewd humor, flights into psychoses and oratory, and fishing—these were their ways of escape.

A poverty-making pattern of life had slid as softly as cotton, inch by inch, across the region, smothering men's hearts and minds and bodies.

⤙ Part Four ⤚

The Dream and Its Killers

⌐ 1 ⌐

Man Against the Past

IT HAS been a long sorrowful story of failure and frustration and anxiety, a tale of shattered lives and a shattered culture that I have told here, made of pages out of history and memories out of childhood.

But there have also been triumphs. There was too much that is good and creative and sane in our people for our appointment in Samarra to be kept and finally we turned back from that journey towards destruction that had wasted not only our region's land but its mind and spirit.

It was a slow journey back home and not easy for our people to make, for we had lived in our never-never land so long. We had worn our invisible crinoline skirts with such charm; we had rested our powers of observation so comfortably behind old white columns that had crumbled or never been built; we had wandered down fabulous magnolia-shadowed driveways where only Chinaberry trees had grown; we had ridden to hounds though most of us did not own even a mule to plow with; all of us, no matter if we had only a tin spoon with which to shovel in grits and fatback, no matter how weak with pellagra and rickets, had eaten wondrous southern cooking all of our lives off of old buried silver that the Yankees had stolen. Our life had been, as politicians even

now tell us, the "best life anyone has ever lived on this
earth." Only last year the *Textile Bulletin* of Charlotte, N.C.,
reaffirmed our good fortune, stating ". . . nowhere do the
yellow race or the black race live upon a higher plane than
the lowest divisions of the white race."

It was hard for people used to such mythic grandeur to return to a life of plain facts. But, though we were stunned at
the crude notion of men testing out with their senses and
scientific technics these matters which our wishful "logic"
had proved to be true with no testing at all, that unknown
southern region, Reality, was being explored at last. Fact
was piled on fact, and still the social scientists kept explor-
ing. There seemed nothing too sacred in Dixie, nothing too
small, to be measured and counted and touched and looked
at: churches and mill town, the soil and the shanties, crops
and incomes. It was a poor substitute for fantasy, this new
diet of facts, but gradually we accepted it, though for a long
time the word "sociology," said with a southern accent, made
a hissing sound of scorn in our ears.

But once the old conspiracy of silence was broken, once
the refusal to look at things as they are had weakened, a few
hungrily read the books that told us the things we already
knew but which we had rarely spoken aloud. And we learned
our facts about poverty and ignorance and eroded soil and
waste, and formed organizations to meet the needs that these
facts made plain to us. But resistance to change piled high. It
was made the foundation of political platforms; it was sometimes the text for sermons; it gave us our most eloquent editorials. Ramparts of phrases were thrown up to block our return to the world we had rejected, but somehow the journey
continued.

We made great errors, as do all groups in times of change.
We confused means with ends. The best of us sometimes exploited people for what we called "social goals." We found it

hard to take criticism with grace though we often secretly profited from it. Politicians skillfully turned our attention to Russia and Germany and Harlem whenever we began to look too closely at our own region. And we let them, glad to be eased from the weight of our own sins.

Though all three seemed equally heinous, as politicians described them, it was Russia that stirred us most deeply. Russia the unknown, Russia the terrible, looming in front of us like a great mountain blocking old familiar paths. Few southerners were familiar with that eerie story of a people's revolt against czarism, whose first chapter began with so fine a concern for the welfare of the people though even then it was stained by fierce violence and was followed by those sickening second and third chapters in which idealism rotted in blood and intolerance and fear until finally it died and became only manure out of which sprang evil and dangerous growths of "dictatorship," "police state," "liquidation" of men. Few southerners understood this but they hated communism because it was a new way of sinning when the old ways of sinning were good enough for us; it was a new way of making and using money; it was a new concern with people. It was change. It seemed to mean that workers were no longer just "hands," and in their minds southerners tied communism up with labor unions and high wages for both were new in the South; and their politicians tied it fast to every manifestation of concern for people's welfare and every movement that might limit their own power, and to everything that might make it more difficult for them to win an election; while the churchmen tied it up with psychoanalysis, and "free love" and hostility to the church. Communism to our people was confusion, and confusion is a powerful weapon with which to lacerate the mind and to fill it with terror.

But the more liberal of southerners were not frightened

by the menace of the Communists, knowing a menace closer home. Nor were we seduced by communism itself. We had struggled too hard to free ourselves from Southern Tradition to creep now under the coat of Russian Tradition. We feared being dictated to, having been dictated to so long by a force in the South that is as vague, as invisible, and almost as successful in making southerners conform as is the party line for Communists; we had fallen in love with freedom for all men regardless of race, in a land of white supremacy, and could not give it up to any party or group anywhere in the world. How could we forgive Russia its iron curtain, its putting of state rights above human rights when we opposed with all our heart and mind and skill the states' righters of our own South! Segregation was too much our mortal enemy—and to make it so we had been compelled to break too many childhood chains and sometimes the hearts of those we loved— for us to tolerate segregation in any of its communist disguises. We had learned the hard way to be loyal to belief in the dignity of man and the honor of the individual. It was not easy to bribe us with a few quick "social goals." Having learned to look at the faults of this South where we were born, we could not blind ourselves to the sins of Russia to which we had no deep ties at all.

Then came the New Deal. And change, like mounted policemen, pressed us down the crowded years. Yet despite the severe adjustments required of us, race conflicts were not as acute as one might have predicted. The New Deal gave the poorer white so much that he needed that for a time there was little room left in his heart for the resentment against the Negro race that a few comfortable folk on Main Street and in governors' mansions had tried to stir up. Food in stomachs, WPA jobs, a little money in the pocket, the NYA training centers, adult education classes, FSA, gave to our people not an understanding of human relations but a temporary tolerance, as bland and undifferentiated as a well-fed dry-diapered baby feels toward the world that surrounds it.

But when the war years came, the tolerance faded. There was more money than our South had ever seen before, higher wages, more jobs, better prices for crops, yet anxiety was on the increase in the southern mind. There was talk during the war of a mass revival of the Klan; there were shocking outbursts of race hatred in the speeches of southerners in Congress, and in state legislatures. Political candidates were building platforms on hate, and the poor and ignorant were expressing an unformulated anxiety in sudden outbursts of lynchings and violence. Though prejudice fattens on poverty and ignorance, it was obvious that prosperity does not inevitably bring with it a commensurate esteem for human rights. Yet we heard more often than ever before, in South and North, that the cause of racial prejudice is economic. The Marxists had been good teachers; even so, their stork story would never have been believed had there not been a need in our people to believe it. They were compelled either to believe that economics brought race prejudice or find out where prejudice comes from.

And since they had already guessed, they did not want to know. In spite of trying not to listen to the lessons psychoanalysis was teaching the world about hostility and self-destruction, and guilt and anxiety, and love and hate, many of our people had heard them. Compared to Sigmund Freud— who was feared as much by Communists and Nazis as by white supremacists—Karl Marx looked like an indulgent big brother. Even so, it was an ambivalent relationship for though race prejudice was "economic," the only form of economics that our people would accept was capitalism. . . .

Not overnight, but slowly, almost imperceptibly the Negro had changed from "the white man's burden" to "the Negro problem"; and from "the Negro problem" to "a minority problem"; and then in a lightning-quick change, men were saying that the "problem" is that of the white man. Suddenly, the Negro race was no longer on the defensive, compelled by cold-eyed skeptics to prove itself "equal" to the white race. Anthropologists had gone to great pains to "prove" that the differences between races are negligible as compared to the differences between individuals of the same "race," and had stressed, like an anxious school teacher, the fact that it is culture, not "chromosomes," that makes some of our most vaunted differences; and that culture is not inherited but first learned in the family. And then it began to dawn on us that only a paranoid or criminal mind could comfortably demand such proof anyway. "What does *equality* mean?" people asked themselves. And a few whispered, "What does it matter?" Suppose one man is "superior" to another in one or more ways—what privilege does that give him save the opportunity to use his talent in creative interesting ways? What relevance can "equality" have in a concept of human rights that is built on a belief in the dignity of every child and his freedom to grow?

Shocked to the bone, we began to perceive that the white race was now on the defensive. The mirrors of the world were turned on us and we did not like what we saw there.

I think it was a feeling, often unverbalized, that a profound change was sweeping across the whole earth and no one could escape it, that began to stir a new anxiety in men's minds. It is a hard thing to think quietly when one is in panic. Then it is that we seize the stereotyped questions that have grown up through the years, and use them as a shield to ward off fear. And they were used by white people everywhere—those questions we all know having to do with sex and segre-

gation, with culture and chromosomes, with time, with a
curious deliberate confusion of our public and private rights
—used stubbornly, desperately, to block off the future which
we could see so plainly when we looked.

But the more thoughtful were searching for insight, and
questioning their own souls, and struggling to find a way out
of trouble for our people. Ministers, church women, little
magazines, fact-finding groups, more and more books, more
and more decisions from the U.S. Supreme Court glowing
with human justice stirred the southern conscience as never
before in history.

Almost by the sheer weight of words the old southern mold
had cracked wide open and we were looking at ourselves inside it. We were exposed to our own image, seeing for the
first time, many of us, our selves as persons. And seeing, we
reached out, and tentatively touched our infantilisms;
weighed the hate and guilt in our hearts; peered down into
the deep chasm that has split our ideals from our acts, slowly
began to realize that anxiety, not love, dominates our lives,
that greed and machines are too often our substitute for
tender human relationships, that we are more comfortable
with fantasy than with the truth. We looked in the mirror
that our Age of Information had turned on us and saw not
Superman, as we believed ourselves to be, but a child whose
teeth were chattering as night drew near. It was as if we, like
Alice, had drunk a liquid and had begun to shrink in stature
smaller and smaller and smaller. . . .

And of course we could not endure the sight. Had we
looked longer, had we given ourselves time to get used to the
image reflected there, we would have seen that though we
are not as tall as mountains, we are tall enough for men; that
though we do not surpass the rest of the world in intelligence
and maturity and in love and quality of "blood," we have
ample capacity for growth; and though we have almost killed

our dream, we are still dreamers and the dream will never die as long as there is on earth one man left to dream it. But we did not see quite that far. We saw only—though we could not yet admit it—that our burden, that burden which our fathers had believed to be the "colored races," was our own past, that the heavy weight that lay on our hearts was our own childhood, that the change we felt unable to make was a change in ourselves. We were beginning to see at last what the white man's false beliefs about sin and sex and segregation had done to the minds and spirits of the most powerful nation on earth.

There were few among us strong enough, mature enough, objective enough to endure such stark knowledge. And, as a child or a man resists even a slight touch on a raw nerve, as the mentally ill resist the probing of the real, and forgotten, cause of anxiety, so we as a people South—and North—began to resist these new insights.

We used all the well-known technics of resistance that the human mind has developed to ward off self-knowledge. The more ignorant and dishonest of us used the scapegoat method, blaming our troubles, if we were southern, more on the damyankee; if we were northern more on the Communist. Many used the diversion method, projecting their guilt on to other sinners and deeply concerning themselves with British imperialism and India's freedom, or with anti-Semitism in Europe; or with everybody else's lack of religion. And many, more intelligent and honest, kept their eyes closer home and selected out of our milieu, poverty as the "basic" cause of our trouble. If we can just get more unions, give people higher wages, more jobs, more housing, more production, more votes, more things, more cover crops, they said, our troubles will take care of themselves. You might have thought, if you listened only casually, that the kudzu vine was the answer to all problems of human relationships. What we need, people

said—who had called "bolshevik" those experts first suggesting it—are diversified crops, contour plowing, better terrac-
ing, better grasses, more crops of pulpwood, better breeds
of cattle, better freight rates, and a small industry in every
town. What the Negro needs, they said—and many Negroes
agreed with them—are bigger schoolhouses and more school
books and "the vote" and more jobs. If we had all this, if we
had a lot of *things*, they said, the "Negro problem" and anti-
Semitism would disappear—and with them, everybody
hoped, would go also, in a magic way, alcoholism, ill-health,
greed, mental illness, juvenile delinquency, hate and guilt
and dullness of heart and the old old need to be led like
sheep.

Shocked out of our preoccupation with the past by that
naked glimpse we had caught of ourselves in the flashing
mirrors, many of our healthiest people got busy, showing
themselves and their neighbors what can be done to worn-
out soil when one has a will to do it. And magnificent things
were done. Many of the activities were simple daily tasks
concerned with improving our patterns of farming, but now
and then a project was of fabulous and dramatic proportions
as was the Winder Experiment, which made over a worn-out
farm in a day.

It was a big step ahead, along that rugged steep road to recovery. It was good occupational therapy.

But we were still bending to the power of southern tradition though thoughtful parents had begun to suspect that
this filthy old procuress who supports politicians and their
industrialist-backers has far too much to do with shaping the
lives of our children.

There were still laws on statute books to make it illegal for
children to grow into mature human beings: laws forcing
little white children to the front, little colored ones to the
rear of buses, sending them through White and Colored

doors, compelling them to inflict and accept shame, tearing their ideals from their acts each time they go into public places.

And we had not yet, as a region, found the strength to make the stark decision to give up segregation, though more and more southerners had begun to see it as a crime against the human spirit, and more and more churches and religious organizations have taken a stand against it.

We had not yet answered the questions of that troubled young girl who wanted to know why parents teach ideals that cannot be lived unless laws are broken, why Christianity is cherished when it is not believed in, and why tradition is so powerful that no one dares offend it. And we had not yet met the needs of our rural people that have to do with homes and health and recreation or their spiritual needs that have to do with the concept of human relations.

Though we were working hard, in our efforts to solve problems of human relations by solving them economically we had made a kind of Faustian bargain; we were whispering to our conscience that if we rebuild our gullied eroded soil maybe, just maybe, we shall not have to rebuild our gullied eroded souls and minds. If we change things, rearrange them, acquire more of them, maybe, somehow, we can once more avoid disaster without changing ourselves.

And perhaps we could have got by for a few years longer, had not the atom bomb been dropped on Hiroshima on August 6, 1945. Maybe time would have been our ally had not that fatal day turned time into our mortal enemy.

It was as if the whole world overnight had run up its clocks a hundred years. Walls fell. Barriers crumbled. Distances snapped together like a piece of elastic. Color, race, religion, nationality no longer had relevance. We were just people, two and one-third billion frightened people, clinging to one small earth which could give us no protection against the hate in men's heart and this dread power in their hand.

I do not know how any other person felt when he heard that the bomb had been dropped. I know only the sudden feeling in me of a vacuum—as if all the past had rushed out and no future would dare creep in. There was not even fear, or guilt; there was Void.

It was too big. Too much knowledge. Too sharp a break with the past. Too terrible a crime that man had committed against himself. We had been forced into a future that our feelings had no preparation for and our minds could grasp only crude approximations of. The scientists by their awesome success and their awesome failure had shot us like a rocket into a world yet unformed.

And after a gasp, a shrill moment of terrified exclamation, we tried to deny. We slammed doors in our mind; we scratched August 6 off of the world calendar; we began to build wispy shaky bridges to tie us to a past that no longer was there. We began to throw up thin trembling walls that could no more shut out danger than a piece of paper can stop a fire but would serve only for a brief moment to shut out the sight of the future we were already in the center of.

People in panic began to gravitate toward their own kind, following the pattern of their life that began long ago when they were small children. White supremacists, Communists, liberals . . . your friends, your family even, parted company with you and each other and began their journey, dotted with ideological road signs, which led each so inevitably to his own psychological destination.

In panic, we, the people, were on our way. Blinded by our big slogans we were crashing into each other—there was no way to see the sharp curves ahead so cluttered was the road with signs urging us to detour from the future.

The war between nations had ended and the war with ourselves had begun.

2

We Are Tall Enough for Men

TODAY, confusion encircles the world. Fascist fighting with liberal against Communist; Communist fighting with liberal against Fascist; liberal fighting liberal; white supremacist fighting the Communist; men believing the same things fighting each other to death for different reasons; men believing in different things becoming allies against those who share their own beliefs.

It is a vast cyclorama of errors. Men, afraid because they cannot see, struggle with each other across an earth strewn with the symbols of man's broken faith with himself: concentration camps and Jim Crow, firing squads and the KKK, Dachau and burning crosses, NKVD, mental hospitals, starving children, and in the foreground the most gruesome trials that the world has known since the Inquisition. It is as if every one of us has made himself a Grand Inquisitor and is trying the whole world for heresy. And all the world will be found guilty, for we have betrayed the human spirit, and deep in our minds we know that of all acts this is the most treasonable. No wonder men drive each other to take loyalty oaths, try each other's beliefs, and find everyone guilty of what they themselves have done.

For we have forgot our dream of the strong, free human being. We have forgot that man is the end of all human endeavor; that the ballot, the job, the wages, the housing are only means to this end. In this time of change, we have lost the free man who can bring change about in his own mind where all change must begin.

We have forgot so much. We have forgot that democracy is the only political faith on earth, the only way of life, that depends for its success on the quality of the men within it. Kings, once wielding sovereign power, did not care about increasing the stature of the human being, for they wanted no man as tall as themselves. Communism would be deeply embarrassed by maturity in its party members and human growth would be a crime against the state. Fascism, like communism, is willing to reward its citizen-slaves with things, but dignity is not in a Fascist's vocabulary nor is human integrity in his code.

We have forgot that democracy is not based on bargains in which big ends are surrendered to small goals, but is based on a concord of belief in the common man's uncommon soul and in the child's capacity for growth. When men share such a belief as to what is democracy's final end, compromise on means by which goals may be brought about is a reasonable method to use—if these goals do not diminish the human being for whom they have been set up. Though too many forget it, this is democracy's way. There is no finality, no carrying of matters to their logical end; there are inconsistencies, and humor; there is a wide margin for error; and yet always there is awareness that though a man's feet are rooted in the earth this limitation is no reason for blinding his eyes so that the stars cannot be seen.

Most important of all, we have forgot that the future is man's. Whatever it is, however it shapes itself up, it belongs to the human being. He is its center: his child's growth is its first concern, his freedom is its major obligation, its institutions must protect his dignity and his life.

We forget these things, as the storm of change tears to pieces our past and flings it around us, taking with it sometimes our most prized symbols, our most cherished fantasies, stripping naked our secrets, making no more than broken matches the patterns of living that we had thought as durable as time.

No one has escaped confusion. But it is the confusion of liberals that I am concerned with, for no matter what labels they pin on themselves they are the carriers of the dream. They will make the future, or the human being will have none. For they and only they have held on to a belief that man is more important than his institutions. It is they who refuse to let him become a slave to his own logic; who know that though he is his own end he never arrives there. And it is they who value his life.

But today liberals are destroying each other. Broken into fragments they seek strength by tying themselves to Fascist groups and Communist groups, and only a few stand on their own feet and boldly declare that the ground is firm beneath them.

They are confused by the seductive lure of things. Things are so easy to make in this Age of Production. Men are so hard to grow. The best of us has been betrayed by the drug-like comfort that things for a time can give the body of man. Knowing the desperate need of hundreds of millions who have never had that minimum of things that keeps men strong enough to hold on to their humanity, certain liberals join forces with Communists, believing that, by doing so, they can the more quickly get these things for all men. Others, shocked at the cheap regard which communism has for the human spirit join forces with any and all "enemies of communism" believing that to "get rid of communism" is the liberal's first task. Too few recognize that authoritarianism is our worst enemy, wherever it springs up, even in our hearts.

Confusion arises because we forget that man's feelings give him his quality; that his physical needs cannot be separated from these feelings about himself; that whatever happens to him happens to the whole of him.

There are two gestures that men make, out of which they create their dance of life: acceptance, withdrawal. Acceptance of life . . . withdrawal into death. We choose. If we accept, we grow; if we withdraw, we die. As we withdraw, we lose our vitality. Starving for those human relationships that we have turned away from, we, like little dirt-eating children, seize upon substitutes. But there is no nourishment for the spirit in them, and finally, we keep our ancient appointment with destruction. It is an old story, told again and again through the ages, about men and about nations.

And yet, though in their hearts they know better, liberals try to believe sometimes that this is not so. They have not quite seen that to accept and to be accepted is the fundamental need of both child and man. And because this is so, they have not given enough thought to the philosophy and pattern of withdrawal and rejection that we call *segregation*.

For nearly a century the South has failed to face the implications of this word. Our nation is failing to do so today.

And because of this failure, democracy may fail to take root in the rich virgin soils of the earth that are plowed and ready for seeds to be planted.

Survival as free men requires that we meet many problems of food, jobs, production, health that confront the whole world today, meet them quickly and meet them squarely, but because human dignity is the essence of free men's belief about themselves we must face this problem first. We must see to it that every man on earth is given his civil rights and we must do it quickly if man the human being is to win his fight against totalitarianism. This is a stern necessity that we must bow to.

A sense of worth, freedom, esteem are what men want most in all the world, and if democracy does not offer it to them, they will take communism. They will choose communism not because it gives them shoes and bread, not because they can live as free men under its regime but because they are accepted on an equal basis. Communism gives them not freedom, not dignity, but "equality." It is the equality of slaves in bondage to a state; but color does not matter there, race does not matter, religion does not matter. The old masks that men across the earth have fought against for the past three centuries are discarded in communism. There is a mask and a terrible one. But as yet its terrors have not been recognized by those longing for acceptance which they have never had. Simple, plain acceptance. And wanting acceptance as human beings they confuse it with the spurious thing called *equality*.

There lies the confusion: in this word *equality*. Men are not equal; they can never be equal in ability, nor in strength nor in health nor in talent nor in size. Men are not alike; they are different. And it is their differences, their infinite variety that democracy honors. Democracy's virtue and strength lie in its willingness to make room for all men however different they are and to provide full opportunity for their growth, permitting each to develop along the lines of his potentialities as an individual. Democracy gives a man freedom to grow, not freedom to keep others from growing.

We in America—and men across the earth—have trapped ourselves with that word *equality* which is inapplicable to the genus *man*. I wish we would forget it. Stop its use in our country. Let the Communists have it. It isn't fit for men who fling their dreams across the skies. It is fit only for a leveling down of mankind. There is only one time when men are equal and that is when they are dead.

Equality is a word, therefore, that has nothing to do with life. But *freedom* glows with life. *Dignity* is a word that gives life worth. *Acceptance* gives life its warmth. *Growth* is life itself. These are words that are made for democratic tongues to say.

We thought up this lie that all men are equal to combat an uglier lie which declared that all men of white color are superior to men who are not white—and its variations: that all men holding a certain religion or opinion are superior to those who do not hold it.

Today, these two lies are trying to divide the world between them. The old battle of epicycles is once more being fought.

We who are comfortable in this uncomfortable world can sit quietly down and discuss matters of semantics; but starving men, humiliated, bruised, frightened, tired men mutely take what is promised them today *if it is only different from their experiences with white supremacy* which two thirds of the earth tremble in anger at the memory of. Any conditions of survival will be accepted by these people if they themselves are accepted. Camaraderie is a powerful lure whether men experience it in the foxholes of war, in the soviets in

Russia, in the Ku Klux Klan, in the Communist party in New York, in Tammany Hall, or out on the golf course.

Liberals must confess that they themselves have not always accepted the rest of mankind. They too have been confused by the word *equality*. Secretly knowing men are not equal, puzzled by this knowledge which seemed in a sense to conflict with their belief in the worth of the human being and his freedom, they retreated to a position of *noblesse oblige*. Even today, they too often substitute paternalism for camaraderie. They will gladly give a man in need their coat if only they do not have to rub shoulders with him. Not for a moment do they think that to give a citizen his civil rights entails giving him one's daughter—no liberal confuses the public rights of men with their private right to control their own personal relationships—but too many have failed and are failing now to identify themselves with all men as human beings. And because of this, the Communists are winning the race for the hearts of men. While the white man in America withholds from colored fellow-citizens the courtesy title of *Mister*, Communists the world over are saying, "Comrade, just call me by my first name."

Perhaps the dilemma is symbolized in this matter of what we call one another: communism levels all men down to the anonymity of first names; democracy raises all up to the dignity of *Mister;* but white supremacy says, "You call me *Mister* and I'll call you *boy.*" And the colored people of the world are remembering.

There is a great hunger in men under stress to be told what to do. As the little child-rebel in trouble runs back to its mother for help, as a grown-up who has lost his strength leans on another, so do men in times of change regress to the infant that hides in all of us, and beg the world for an authority to command them.

Today, there is not one of us who secretly does not want to be told what to do, though we may bravely reserve the right to be critical of the teller, and though we may cravenly refuse to do it after we know.

But we cannot wisely agree on action until we agree on three bases of human conduct: *what we want, what is right,* and *what survival requires of us.*

For thousands of years these three forces have pulled and torn men and civilizations to pieces. No one of them can be dealt with sanely out of context with the other two, even in one personality—how then can we expect other than great difficulty when dealing with them in that composite we call "a people."

The fourth element of agreement is *timing*: the art of recognizing the luminous moment when men's imaginations see alike, and their skill can be pooled in a strategy that piles up, in quick rhythmic succession, effort on effort on effort, until finally in orgastic flowering, the whole body-politic is made one in feeling, belief, desire, act.

In the past these forces seemed always to be pulling against each other. Today, this is no longer true.

Never in all the world's history has it been so easy as now for men to harmonize ideals, desires, reality. For once, the currents are flowing in the same direction. Perhaps they have always flowed in the same direction; the trouble was, that men could not see; and had they seen, would not have had the tools and technics to act. Distance and darkness had to be got rid of before men could see. Walls had to fall, not only between nations and races but in men's own minds. Now they are down. Now men have the tools, the technics, the means to do what needs to be done. This is common knowledge. Our dilemma is that men still think there is conflict between what they want, what is right, and what survival requires of them when actually this is not so.

Each of us wants, I think, to live as a free man, well fed and housed and clothed but free to grow, to make choices, to ask questions, to follow our own interests, to do work that we are fitted to do. We want to be esteemed by our fellows and to respect our own souls; we want to be contrary sometimes and differ with others and change things around. But we want above all else to be free of anxiety, to be loved and cherished, and to dream and bring forth our dream.

Now what does survival require of us? Is it so different that we shall have to give up these desires in order to live?

Communism, today, says *yes*. Communism tells us that in order to have the shoes and roof and loaf of bread we must give up the freedom of mind and spirit and act; that we must do work that the state tells us to do, not that which fits into our talents and inner needs; that we can esteem only the state and must give up the luxury of esteem for each other and ourselves; that not only must we relinquish our need to change things around but above all else we must be full of anxiety, despairingly fearful, so that we shall watch each other and betray each other in order to cajole the powers that are above us. Communism tells us that there is no time and place for the dreamer, that only by giving up the dream can man have the things he wants for his body. And fascism, whose whispers are soft but powerful these days, echoes these things. And Dixiecrats say them also in part, in southern accents, and Republicans have been known to say them, and the church at its worst and certain Socialists and even liberals say words that sound curiously as if they too believe— at least in part—that these conditions are valid on which man is asked to surrender his sovereignty in order to live or to let the power that controls him live.

They tell us—each power in its own way tells us—that survival depends on our relinquishing our status as human beings.

The incredible thing is that so many people believe them. The dangerous thing is that so many American leaders believe them, in Congress, in state legislatures, in high places where public opinion is formed, and are urging our nation to use Russia's methods in order to "fight" Russia. And so a race begins between two powers. . . .

We believe this dangerous nonsense because we have not yet looked at reality—reality, not as it was ten years ago or a thousand but as it is now.

For thousands of years, reality was a vague flat Earth, around which stars and planets swung; dark and distant were people on it, and strange to each other's minds. Walls were everywhere, invisible sometimes, but there. Distance was measured by a man's legs, darkness by a candle, ignorance and fear were holy and a man's mind was as vague as his earth, and as unknown.

And then came Copernicus and the lights began to turn on, one by one by one. After him came other scientific giants, more and more of them, who with the new method called science, in four brief centuries stretched time and the universe to an infinity of light years and bent them back again, split matter into invisible atoms and made each a restless world, expanded man's age a half million years and reduced him to a cell . . . quadrupled the known area of his earth, enhaloed it with an antiquity beyond the oldest dream, raised its production and population to unreckoned levels and then squeezed it into a sphere so tight and small that a whisper could be heard from end to end of it and a journey made from East to West as simply as once from village to village. In four brief centuries these miracles of knowledge came to pass.

Even now, we are not used to these great blinding arcs of light thrown across the old darkness. Even now we grow afraid as we look. But we see where we are. We know now that our everyday world consists of a small earth on which live two billion and a half people who listen to the same radio, often read the same papers, and judge each other's daily actions, as neighbors have always done. We know if any of these people begin to die in large numbers, we all begin to die. Bacteria or atom bombs—what difference! Neither can be contained behind walls, nor does either know the difference in white skin or colored, Christian, Moslem, Hindu, or Hebrew ways of worship or political ways of talking. If any of these people starve in large numbers then we all begin to starve; for crops depend upon markets and markets depend upon people who eat; or we begin to die, for though we grow fat on too much food while China, India, Europe starve, the loaf we refused to cast on the waters comes back to us with inexorable promptitude in the form of epidemics which, fattening first on the people we refused to feed, sweep across our own greedy land. So these things go. Bread and bacteria and bombs packaged together.

We know too that fear and hate, once contained in a man's own heart or known only to those of his family, now set off fear and hate across the world in a chain reaction that explodes, rocking the earth we live on. This is today's reality. Earth and man interacting on each other. Each dependent upon the other; every man leaning on his neighbor and at the same time supporting him.

We know now that what is inside a man has suddenly become important to all other men's survival. Once what was inside a man was as unexplored as the tiny earth we live on. Men did not know that man is round and whole like the earth, and time and space. For those who had power had split him into three flat pieces: body, soul, mind, with fathomless chasms between, and then had split his body into good and evil regions. And to keep these fragments apart—a difficult thing, for there was an irresistible urge toward fusion—they walled each of them away from the other and made it a sin to cross the boundaries. All in man's nature that did not seem "good" to the authorities was pushed outside the little cosmogony and banished into the Lower Depths. And theologians warned us that we would follow these feelings—if we cared too much for them—and become reunited with them, after death. They called this place of reunion, Hell.

And this threat of punishment after death was held over men's minds to make them "be good," to compel them to keep the parts of themselves separate, to do what authorities wanted them to do. Love that could have fused man into a whole was dishonored. Fear grew in their hearts, sweeping through them like a great flood. But the war between the fragments of man, between his instinctual needs and his conscience and his sense of himself continued.

After a time, most men gave up trying to make a human being of dignity and stature out of such twisted, torn, bleeding fragments and began instead to create masks to hide their disfigured selves beneath. These masks we made for ourselves seemed always to celebrate a part or attribute of man, either his skin color or his mind or his belief or the way he made his money or a talent or a power which he had stumbled upon; never the whole human being. But men still were not happy, for masks are a poor thing to cover one's shame with, and hurting, they turned and fought each other like wild beasts. Cowering together in identical mask formation they fought against all other mask formations until they were tired and sometimes forgot even to laugh—which had always had the effect of pulling all parts of a man together.

Then, only a whiff of time ago, less than a century, the scientists discovered the interior of man—though long before then, artists and wise men had guessed it. The region so long called Hell, they named the Unconscious and changed its locale from Out There beyond the rim of things to In Here deep down in a man's own heart, and gave it a time-point not in the future but in our own past, though they agreed with the theologians that it was full of powerful and destructive feelings. They began to talk about love that keeps man together, of guilt that tears him apart, of hate that destroys him, of punishment that has no relevance in the concept of a growing human being. They talked of man's wholeness, of a body that is made sick by its beliefs, of beliefs that spring from a sick body, of glands that control feelings and feelings that disrupt glands; they talked of a childhood that follows a man through life and of infantile passions that can tear a grown-up mind to pieces. And they put sex, dishonored so long, back into its ancient place of esteem.

They drew maps of man's body, tried to draw maps of his mind. They argued with each other over these maps and for a time tore man into pieces as ruthlessly as had the theologians. But slowly, gradually, they began to talk of *man undivided*, whose body and mind and feelings are one, interacting upon each other, upon his world and his world upon it. They declared that man against himself cannot live in peace and health. They reunited sex with love and warned of the dangers of its union with hate. They refused to separate his past from his future. They called this timeless man whom they had rediscovered "psychosomatic man"; and talked of his health in terms of bacteria and food and insight and human relationships. Being scientists, moral terms embarrassed them but in their own way they affirmed that man's health and his life depend on his acceptance of himself and others with love and understanding. They reminded us that man can live in health and peace only by keeping himself and his earth undivided.

Men in the past furiously differed on what is "right" because they listened to different authorities each of whom, seeking power, told them what to believe about good and evil. They differed also because "right" rarely seemed to fit in with what they wanted or what reality required of them in order to keep on living. And gradually they split off their morality from the life they felt compelled to live and sometimes made little attempt to act out their beliefs about it. But nevertheless they cherished it.

It is therefore a hard thing for most of us to acknowledge today that the old morality, split into pieces like the cultures it made and was made by, broken into fragments as is this world of ours and man himself, has no relevance for our future. To say this causes some to cry out that one is suggesting that we can do without morals; but this is not so. We can no more exist without values to cherish, than we can live without air to breathe. For it is man's beliefs that make him human, though sometimes, in conflict with his needs, they make him insane. It is belief that has pulled him from his all-fours, belief made concrete that has carried him so far on that fabulous journey called "civilization." But it is also belief that, dying in his heart, has poisoned his spirit; and it is belief that, cherished but not acted out, has drained his strength from him. Belief, exploited, has brought on wars and terrors, filled mental hospitals, crowded jails and concentration camps, crippled and torn and destroyed men and their cultures. Yet man without belief is inconceivable, no matter how badly he misuses it.

Though we cannot live without belief, we can today live only with beliefs that tie together our wants, our survival needs, our ideals and our world. No authority can give them to us though no one of us can find them alone. Based on the wisdom of the past, on the scientific knowledge of the present, they must be grounded firmly on our instinctual needs and wants and the realities of the world we live in today. They must be such that all men can hold them. And yet each of us must find his own beliefs. And finding, each must share them, not because they are "the only right way" but because by doing so we as a human race can finally reach that concord of belief about ourselves and our world that will hold us firmly together.

I believe there are two journeys which every one of us must make: into our own heart, accepting what we find there; and into the world, accepting it as our home.

I believe there are common goals which each of us shares with the rest of the world: to make our earth a place for children to grow; to fight diseases that attack all of us; to create a world government to which every free man can give his loyalty; to rid the earth of hunger and poverty; to make knowledge and men's creation of beauty accessible to all.

I believe that men as human beings must have in common certain values and that these begin with the belief that love is essential to life: functioning as sex, it is necessary not only for procreation of life but for the full health of the human organism; functioning as sympathy, compassion, devotion, willingness to suffer if others can be benefited by it, it gives man his dignity and his grace as a human being. I believe that love is an expanding feeling that reaches out

toward others and helps them find more abundant life; and
that this expansion, this reaching out to people is necessary
for men's health. I believe love gives man his capacity for
acceptance of life's experiences, for understanding (which
brain alone can never give), his tolerance, his generosity,
his strength. This is love, as I see it: an act of the human
spirit reaching out in tenderness and concern toward all
people.

I think moral values are also concerned with hate—that
emotional excretion of human relationships which, unless
wisely used will destroy men's spirit. I do not believe hate
can be "forbidden" any more than one can forbid the human
body to excrete its waste products. But once accepted as a
natural function, hate can be used as the energy it actually
is in all activities that build and create the good, and in
those that stamp out evil.

I believe there are two giant immoralities of our age, the
more important of which is that hate has been used not only
to destroy life and natural beauty and man's creations that
are good but that it has become tied up with the sex drive,
twisting this life energy to its own cruel uses so that our
times are blazing with sex murders, rapings, KKK, cruelty
in marriage relations, bombings of children in war, and cold
indifference to millions of them now shelterless and hungry
and lonely in peace; and I believe this happened because we
have dishonored love and made childhood a burden too
heavy for grown-up men to bear.

I believe the second of these giant immoralities is the use
of scientific knowledge against man's welfare. Like sex,
knowledge is good if used in the service of life and love. It
is a good thing when it increases man's understanding of
himself and the world he lives in, when it extends his skills,
creates beauty and comfort for him. I believe that atomic

energy is the most significant discovery in man's physical world since men discovered fire, but I believe the fact that its first use was against man himself only dramatizes in a shocking way the truth that men cannot escape their human responsibilities in science any more than they can in politics or in business or in art or in their personal relationships. I believe our big moral problem in this atomic age is concerned with how to grow in men a conscience mature enough, inclusive enough, to meet the needs of all men on earth; and I believe an eight-year-old conscience, which is all most men have to rely on in these troubled times, is as much a hazard to the world's future as are the handful of ruthless exploiters who are striving to control these men.

And I believe our heaviest responsibility is to hold firm to a faith that one's belief is worth working for and one's values are worth living.

This is my "world view." Each of us has to make his own. And yet each must be made in terms of all.

What we do today cannot be decided upon until we agree on these three things: our wants, our survival needs, our belief as to what is right. As for timing? There is no choice. It has to be now.

There are many who will reject so simple a picture as I have given here of man and his world. Preferring to lose themselves in complexities and infinite details, they cannot persuade themselves that "the realities" can be stated in such simple terms as this picture suggests. Confronted with lethal weapons which are so massive in projection of man's feelings of hate and fear, faced with the ambitions of a handful of men who control so much power, they cannot believe in the power of love. They are ashamed of the word. They are of an age that cannot easily define it. They cannot confess that it can conquer the hate and fear in men's minds, that with insight it can block this road to destruction which we in our panic are rushing down at so rapid a pace. These critics, calling themselves "realists," fix their eyes on a world that no longer exists, on needs that have evaporated, on values too fragmentary to be valid for men and insist that we attend to the tasks in front of us with our eyes on the past.

Some of these tasks which we all agree must be accomplished have to do with bodily needs; others are of a symbolic significance. Short-range or far-range, concerned with body or spirit, not one of them can be successfully dealt with unless we accept our future for what it is. But all can be met if we do so, for none is beyond the intelligence of men; none requires more resources of technological skills and knowledge than we possess.

We Americans are perhaps the most flexible people on earth. Nowhere else are people so easy with each other, so free, and resilient. Nowhere is there less awe of authority, less bending to tradition, even though we acknowledge the lag of the South in these particulars. Nowhere more ingenuity and resourcefulness and energy and laughter, nowhere more genuine belief in men's capacity to get what they want, and nowhere are lines so fluid, so everchanging. Nowhere so much wealth, economic power, technological development. Nowhere such potentials for world leadership.

And yet, again and again we let the world down by our moral impotence.

Here lies our weakness: this profound cleavage in our culture and in our people. Distance and darkness and ignorance and fear collaborated so long on this ritual of separation within and without that it is difficult for many to believe today that man divided against himself is not a natural thing.

And now at last, the dreamers who have dreamed so much that is good and beautiful, so much that has increased the stature of man and made his life rich and abundant, have dreamed also the weapon that can destroy all dreams and all men. It is as if man has found the ultimate in evil and can save himself from it only by finding the ultimate in good.

A little crazy hypothesis was once thrown across a dark sky and left there. But no one could ever forget it. Religions were built by its light, poets' minds shone in its brightness, political systems used its warmth to draw men closer together, science cautiously examined it and "proved it" to be the essence of sanity, the seed of human growth. It may be only a bedtime story that men for thousands of years have told themselves in their loneliness. It may be a lie, this sanctity of the human being, this importance of man the individual, this right of the child to grow, but when it is proved so, there will no longer be an earth to witness the lie's triumph and no men here to mourn the loss of their dream.

Man . . . with feet tied to the past and hands clutching at the stars! Only by an agonizing pull of his dream can he wrench himself out of such fixating stuff and climb thin air into the unknown. But he has always done it and he can do it again. He has the means, the technics, he has the knowledge and insight and courage, he has the dream. All have synchronized in beautiful harmony, for the first time in his history. Does he have the desire? That is a question that each human being must answer alone. It is a secret ballot that one by one we shall cast, and only those votes will be counted that are cast in time.